RETIRING PROCRASTINATION BEFORE TOMORROW

What is it and how to prevent it
by Staying Productive, Fulfilled
and Happy in Retirement

GAVIN RANKIN

DISCLAIMER

This book is written and intended for educational or informational purposes only. The content presented in this book is not a substitute for legal, financial, medical, professional, or other advice. Any reliance placed by the reader on any of the content of this book is strictly and entirely at the reader's own risk.

ISBN: 978-1-0686986-3-7 - (Paperback)

ISBN: 978-1-0686986-1-3 - (eBook)

ISBN: 978-1-0686986-2-0 - (Hardback)

To my dearest wife of many years who always knew what to do and when and how to do it, always being the main thinker and solution finder, who led by example and never ever put off what could be done immediately. She taught me so much over our time together, for which I will always be extremely grateful.

To my son and daughter, who have always been my pride and joy, through the many good, and occasional bad times, and for the enduring memories we have shared.

To my beautiful, loving, and caring granddaughter, who is now a young adult, in the hope that one day, long into the future, when she is looking at retirement, she may gain some valuable help and guidance from what this book is all about.

Finally, to my gorgeous great grand-daughter, who at present is far too young to even begin to understand these things, but it is my hope that one day she may become a successful, happy, go-getting, pro-active entrepreneur, who never gives up and always aims for the top in everything that she ever attempts.

BETIRING PROCRASTINATION BEFORE TOMORROW

What is it and how to prevent it by Staying Productive, Fulfilled and Happy in Retirement

CONTENTS

ARE YOU READY?
THEN LET'S GO

INTRODUCTION

Welcome, to a journey into the world of procrastination, but don't roll your eyes just yet. This isn't your typical self-help book filled with rigid rules and chapters you must read in a specific order. No, this book is more like a collection of thoughts, ideas and suggestions where you can nibble on a little here, taste a bit there, and come back for seconds whenever the mood strikes you. There may be one or two suggestions which are vaguely repetitive, perhaps with slightly different emphasis, but that is because they are so important in your efforts to totally conquer any tendency to procrastinate.

So, why was it designed it this way? Because if you're picking up a book on procrastination, the chances are high that you may already be a bit of a procrastinator. The author figured a book that's too structured might just end up collecting dust on your bookshelf, or making a good temporary door stop. Instead, he has tried to create something more flexible, and hopefully, more helpful for you in your bid to avoid procrastinating.

This is not your average read, as it doesn't have to be read from beginning to end, nor should it be. Think of it simply as a collection of index cards or sticky paper notes rather than a linear novel or text book. Each chapter or section stands alone, offering you snippets of suggestions, observations and practical advice about dealing with the tendency to procrastinate. You can start anywhere—yes, anywhere. Feeling like you need a quick pep talk? Jump into any part of any chapter. A basic paper book marker could be useful.

Bite-Sized items within each short chapter or section are self-contained. You get a complete idea or strategy without needing to read the whole book. Perfect for those moments when you have just a few minutes to spare, or you're temporarily at a loss of what to do next; so pick up this book and open it anywhere to get some snippet of encouragement.

Mood-based reading: Some days, you might need a hard-hitting strategy to kick your procrastination habit. Other days, you might just feel like sitting down with a coffee and looking for a way to kill the procrastination that you are not going to get into. Flip to whatever suits your mood. Read what you need, when you need it

The beauty of this book's format is that it's designed to be there for you whenever you need it. No pressure to read it cover to cover. Just dive in, read a section or two, and apply what you've learned. You can always come back later for more.

Flexibility: Life is unpredictable. Maybe you only have time to read while waiting for your coffee to brew. With this book, you don't have to worry about losing track of a complex argument or forgetting key points because you had to put it down suddenly.

Short on time? Some sections offer rapid-fire advice and strategies that you can implement right away. Perfect for a quick read when you're on the go.

After reading a section, take a moment to reflect. Jot down any thoughts, feelings, or actions you want to take. Implement one or two ideas and see how they work for you. The goal isn't to overwhelm yourself but to gradually integrate these strategies into your life. Treat this book as your go-to guide for whenever you feel procrastination creeping in.

Ready to really dig in and tackle your procrastination head-on? Some longer sections provide more detailed ideas and suggestions to help you form better habits.

We know that procrastination isn't just about laziness or poor time management. It's a complex issue influenced by various factors, including fear of failure, perfectionism, and sometimes, plain old habit.

Remember, the path to overcoming procrastination isn't a straight line. It's a quirky, winding road filled with ups and downs. Some days you'll be on fire, knocking out tasks left and right. Other days, you might find yourself binge-watching your favorite series instead of tackling your to-do list. And that's okay. The key is to keep moving forward, even if it's just one small step at a time. With the tips, ideas, and suggestions from this book, you'll have a trusty friend. So, there you have it; a book on procrastination that's anything but traditional.

Whether you're looking for a quick tip, or a deep dive into the psychology of procrastination, you'll find it somewhere within the following pages, and remember, there's no right or wrong way to read this book. Just jump in wherever you feel like, and let your journey begin.

Happy reading, and may your procrastination be vanquished forever, or at least kept at bay.

CHAPTER

1

The detrimental effects of procrastination and the benefits of staying productive in retirement

Retirement is often viewed as a period of life in which, after many years of often highly pressurized or boring hard work, it finally becomes a time for relaxation, leisure, and the freedom to pursue one's own interests instead of those of your now ex-employer.

However, while it's essential to embrace this idea, it is equally important to avoid falling unsuspectingly into a habit of over relaxing to the point of doing nothing at all. This is Procrastination!

Procrastination can have a seriously detrimental effect on a person's well-being, productivity, and overall satisfaction, especially during this significant stage of life.

In this chapter let's explore why procrastination can be particularly harmful in retirement, and look at some steps that can be taken to overcome this tendency and help toward leading a genuinely fulfilling and purposeful life.

Loss of Productivity

Procrastination is notorious for diminishing productivity, and in retirement, this is no exception. With no strict deadlines or external pressures, the retiree may find it tempting to postpone tasks indefinitely. However, this delay can result in a loss of productivity and a growing sense of having achieved nothing. Whether it's pursuing personal projects, engaging in hobbies, or maintaining social connections, productive use of one's time is crucial for any retiree to experience a sense of accomplishment and purpose.

Diminished Mental and Physical Health

Engaging in activities and staying mentally and physically active is vital for a retiree to maintain optimal well-being. Procrastination on the other hand, often leads to sedentary habits and a decline in mental stimulation which can reduce mental ability. This lack of engagement can contribute to feelings of boredom, isolation, and even depression. By actively avoiding procrastination, a retiree can nurture their mental and physical health, leading to a more fulfilling retirement.

Missed Opportunities

Retirement offers an abundance of opportunities for personal growth, learning, and exploration. However, when procrastination takes hold, these opportunities can easily slip away. Whether it's traveling, volunteering, starting a new business venture, or pursuing educational courses, seizing opportunities requires a proactive mindset. Procrastination can hinder a retiree's ability to fully embrace and maximize the potential of their retirement years, leading to regret and a sense of missed chances.

Strained Relationships

Procrastination not only affects individuals personally, but can also strain relationships with one's family, friends, and loved ones. When a retired person continuously delays commitments, fails to follow through on promises, or puts off quality time with others, it can erode trust and lead to feelings of frustration and disappointment. Building and nurturing relationships requires dedication and active participation, both of which can be undermined by procrastinating.

Financial Consequences

Retirement often requires careful financial planning to ensure a comfortable and secure future. However, procrastination in managing one's financial affairs can have severe consequences. Delaying important financial decisions, such as estate planning or investment management, can lead to missed opportunities for growth and protection of assets. Procrastination in financial matters can result in financial stress and a very uncertain retirement outlook.

Overcoming Procrastination in Retirement

Once the possible detrimental effects of procrastination in retirement is properly understood, it's essential to explore a number of ways to overcome this tendency and lead a more fulfilling life.

Set meaningful goals

Establishing some clear and achievable goals can help to provide a sense of purpose and direction, and perhaps give one the motivation to take some action toward getting there.

Prioritize and plan

Set about creating a structured routine and prioritize tasks within it based on their importance. Breaking larger tasks into smaller, manageable steps can make them less overwhelming and more attainable.

Create accountability

Make arrangements to engage in regular check-ins with an accountability partner or join a retirement group that promotes mutual support and encouragement among its members.

Cultivate self-discipline

Develop some habits that will foster self-discipline, such as setting specific timeframes for each task, minimizing any possible distractions, and practicing some mindful techniques to remain on the task in hand.

Embrace lifelong learning

Engaging in continuous learning of some kind and exploring new interests can help one stay mentally stimulated and actively promote personal growth.

The Benefits of staying Productive

Retirement is often seen as a time for relaxation, leisure, and finally being able to enjoy the fruits of one's labor. However, more and more retirees are discovering the benefits of staying productive during this phase of life. Rather than simply settling into a sedentary routine, they are finding renewed purpose, fulfilment, and overall well-being by remaining active and engaged in various activities. In the following pages, we will explore the advantages of staying productive in retirement and how it can positively enhance one's overall quality of life.

Mental Stimulation

One of the main benefits of remaining productive in retirement is the continued mental stimulation it provides. Taking part in activities that challenge the mind, such as learning new skills, pursuing hobbies, or even starting a small business, can help keep the brain sharp and active. This mental stimulation has been understood to be linked to a reduced risk of cognitive decline and can contribute to maintaining good mental abilities well into old age.

Physical Health

Staying productive in retirement often goes hand in hand with maintaining an active lifestyle. Whether it's taking regular walks, participating in fitness classes, or engaging in volunteer work that requires physical exertion, remaining physically active can have numerous health benefits. Regular exercise helps to maintain strength, flexibility, and cardiovascular health, reducing the risk of chronic illnesses and improving one's overall well-being.

Social Connections

Retirement can sometimes lead to a sense of isolation or loss of social connections that were once freely available in the workplace. Staying productive offers a retiree the opportunity to foster new relationships and maintain existing ones.

Engaging in volunteer work, joining clubs or community organizations, or even pursuing some part-time employment can help one stay socially connected and combat feelings of loneliness. Social interactions are crucial for mental and emotional well-being, and staying productive in retirement provides a great platform for meaningful connections with others.

Sense of Purpose

Many individuals take pleasure and derive a sense of purpose from their careers, and retirement can sometimes create a massive void in this aspect of their life. However, staying actively productive in retirement allows a new retiree to discover new sources of purpose and meaning. Whether it's mentoring younger individuals, starting a passion project, or contributing to the community, staying productive helps retirees maintain a sense of purpose, contributing to a greater overall sense of happiness and fulfilment.

Financial Benefits

While retirement is often associated with financial stability and the ability to relax, staying productive can provide additional financial benefits. Engaging in part-time work or turning a hobby into a small business can offer retirees an additional source of income, which can be beneficial for funding travel, pursuing new hobbies, or supporting philanthropic endeavors. Furthermore, staying productive may also delay the need to dip into retirement savings, providing greater financial security for the future.

Retirement is a daunting time of unknown transition, but it doesn't need to be a time of idleness. By staying productive, retirees can enjoy a host of benefits that positively impact their mental, physical, and emotional well-being. Engaging in meaningful activities, maintaining social connections, and finding new sources of purpose can all contribute to a more fulfilling and satisfying retirement. So, instead of merely settling into a life of leisure and relaxation, consider staying productive and embrace the multitude of opportunities that retirement has to offer.

CHAPTER

2

**Understanding Procrastination and
how it can adversely affect our life**

Procrastination is the habit of delaying what needs to be done now, until sometime in the future rather than facing up to it and getting it done. We've all been there, preferring to find something else to do rather than the necessary job that really needs to be done today. But what precisely is procrastination, and why do we engage in this lethargic act of postponement. Let's explore the depths of this damaging behavior.

Defining Procrastination

Procrastination, is the annoying ability to defer a task, assignment, or a responsibility to a later time or date, despite knowing full well that it should be done now and not tomorrow. Something tempts us away from our obligations with thoughts of something else to do instead of the task in hand. We find ourselves concentrating on the allure of Netflix, Amazon Prime, social media, or the desire to rearrange the book case or simply having a little rest. We are quietly, steadily, drawn into any distraction we can possibly think of.

The Causes

Now, one might wonder, why on Earth does one procrastinate when it will only lead to stress and panic later on. Unfortunately, the causes are many and varied like the flavors of ice cream or the available colors of tee shirts.

Let's look at shedding some light on just a few of the many and varied factors.

Instant Relaxation Mode

Deep within the brain, resides part of a divided part of a lobe which, unless one is a brain surgeon, would be impossible to understand, but it works in a mischievous way to hijack our attention. When faced with a daunting task, this little brain part convinces us that relaxing and watching a travel video or perfecting our paperclip collection is far more important than getting on with the job that really needs to be done right now -not later. When this happens, other people think we are procrastinating! We are!

Fear of Failure

The prospect of failure can worry and haunt us like a persistent mosquito or a hard to get at itch. It bothers and fills us with self-doubt and anxiety. Procrastinating, in its peculiar way, becomes a shield, protecting us from the possibility of disappointment. If we don't try, we can't fail, right? Wrong! But try convincing our overprotective subconscious. It's not easy.

Perfectionism Paralysis

Admit it to yourself if you've ever fallen victim to this. Perfectionism can be described as the relentless pursuit of flawless perfection and can lead us down a worryingly lethargic course of inaction. We set impossibly high standards for ourselves, fearing that anything less than perfection is a sign of weakness or inadequacy. so, we delay, and we delay some more, waiting for the right moment to arrive, but it rarely does.

Time Illusion

Time, of course is an unparalleled problem. It plays with our minds, making us believe we have a vast abundance of it when, in reality, it simply slips away like sand. We convince ourselves that we can conquer the world in a day, only to realize that 24 hours are barely enough to tackle a fraction of our to-do list. The result being that we put things off, thinking we have all the time in the world until reality strikes when we realize we now don't have time to do the job anyway.

So, we've set off on a journey to unravel the enigma of procrastination. From the Instant Gratification part of our brain to the ever-present fear of failure, the causes are as diverse as they are problematical.

But luckily, acknowledging the problem is the first step towards overcoming it.

Let's admit our human imperfections and accept that we may sometimes succumb to the temptations of procrastination, but also recognize the importance of stepping out of its grasp. Set realistic goals, break tasks into manageable chunks, and confront the fear that lurks somewhere in the back of our mind. Remember, life is a delicate balance between work and play, and procrastinating will only serve to upset that balance. So, say good bye to the habit of procrastinating and set out on a journey of productivity, one step at a time.

But first of all, perhaps a small break wouldn't be a bad idea. After all, there's plenty of time. Wrong.

How Procrastination affects Retirement

Retirement is that long-awaited time in one's life when the alarm clock is silenced, and you can forever forget the old Monday morning start. It's that wonderful time of leisure and relaxation that you've been looking forward to for all those hard-working years. Let's take a look at how procrastination can affect the lives of those who should be embracing endless free time.

Doing Nothing

In retirement, the temptation to indulge in doing nothing can be very strong. From lounging on the porch with a good book to binge-watching your favorite TV shows, the temptation to be idle becomes ever more inviting. Procrastination creeps in when days turn into weeks, and weeks into months, with a growing but very much untouched to-do list. The saying "Why do today what you can put off until tomorrow?" sadly becomes the norm.

The Promise of Tomorrow

A Retiree can often convince themselves that they have all the time in the world. The thought of endless tomorrows gives an ideal starting point for some procrastinating. That book you've been meaning to write, that exotic holiday destination you've been dreaming of exploring, or the new hobby you've been planning to get involved in, all these can easily fall by the wayside and victim to the comforting promise of "tomorrow". Procrastination thrives on the false hope that time is an infinite resource.

"I might do it later"

Some comfort is perceived in the famous phrase, "I'll do it later." The retirement years seem tailor-made for this procrastinator's anthem. From simple household chores to important life decisions, putting things off becomes the modus operandi. Before you know it, a sea of postponed tasks engulfs your once blissful retirement plans. The laundry pile grows taller, the garden becomes a jungle, and the grand plans for home renovations gather dust on the shelf.

The Internet Black Hole

The virtual labyrinth that is the internet, is where procrastination meets endless time-wasting entertainment. Retirement now provides a huge amount of time to explore the vast depths of websites in all shapes and sizes, and incalculable interests, but it also poses the risk of falling into an inexplicable internet black hole.

From funny cat videos to social media scrolling marathons, the internet becomes a double-edged sword, both a source of invaluable and often useless information, and a dark, unforgiving abyss of procrastination. Time melts away as retirees immerse themselves in the captivating yet ultra time-consuming digital world

The Myth of Productivity

Contrary to popular belief, retirement doesn't automatically transform us into productivity superheroes. While some retirees may find themselves embracing new ventures and ticking off their bucket lists, others succumb to the myth that productivity is a thing of the past. Procrastination takes hold and seizes the opportunity to convince retirees that they've earned their rest, pushing important tasks and personal goals to the side. After all, why bother when retirement is meant for relaxation?

Retirement, that utopia of boundless free time, can become a basis for procrastination if left unchecked. The art of doing nothing, the promise of "tomorrow," the rise of "I'll do it later," the internet black hole, and the myth of productivity all combine to lure retirees into the habit of procrastinating. While there's nothing wrong with enjoying well-deserved leisure, striking a balance between relaxation and taking care of essential tasks and personal aspirations is key.

So, embrace the joy of accomplishing your dreams, even if it means overcoming the temptation to do nothing from time to time. Remember, time is very much a limited resource, and life's adventures await those who can resist the call of "I'll do it later." A happy retirement can be filled with both pleasurable leisure and meaningful pursuits, minus the damaging habit of procrastination!

CHAPTER

3

The Psychology of Retirement

Retirement marks a significant transition in one's life, a period of change that brings both challenges and opportunities. After years of dedicated work and commitment, retirement offers the chance to enjoy the fruits of one's labor and embrace a new and exciting phase of life. However, this transition is not without its complexities. Let us explore the challenges that retirees may face and the opportunities that await them in this new chapter of life.

Loss of Work Identity

For many individuals, work becomes intertwined with their identity. Retirement can, therefore, present a challenge as a retiree adjusts to a life without their familiar professional roles and colleagues. The shift from being a productive member of the workforce to a retiree may result in feelings of having no purpose or a loss of self-worth. It is vitally important to proactively address this challenge by seeking new sources of fulfilment and self-identity beyond the workplace. Retirement provides an opportunity to explore personal passions, hobbies, or even pursue further education. Engaging in meaningful activities, volunteering, or mentoring, can help retirees find a renewed sense of purpose and allow them to contribute to society in new and different ways.

Financial Considerations

One of the most significant challenges a retiree faces is managing their finances effectively. The transition from a regular income to relying on retirement savings and or a pension requires careful planning and adherence to a budget. A Retiree must carefully evaluate their new financial situation, consider healthcare costs, and factor in potential inflation or unexpected expenses.

To overcome these challenges, a retiree needs to develop a comprehensive financial plan. Seeking guidance from financial advisors or retirement experts can be immensely helpful in creating a sustainable retirement plan, but can also be costly if one is not careful where or whom to seek the advice from. It is essential to review one's investments (if any), adjust one's spending habits, and ensure that any retirement savings are aligned with one'slong-term financial goals and aspirations.

Social Changes

Retirement often involves a shift in one's social situation. Colleagues who were once part of a daily routine may no longer be readily accessible, or even not wish to be. The absence of work-related social interactions can lead to a sense of isolation or loneliness. Retirees must adapt to new social environments and build new connections beyond the workplace.

Getting involved in local community activities, joining clubs or interest groups, and participating in volunteer work can foster new friendships and provide a sense of belonging. Embracing technology can also facilitate connections with loved ones and help retirees maintain existing social ties despite any physical distances.

Structure and Routine

The structure and routine provided by work can be a comforting aspect of daily life. Retirement, however, can and probably will disrupt these familiar patterns, leaving a retiree to grapple with newfound free time. The absence of a set schedule may result in a loss of productivity or a lack of motivation, or both.

To overcome this challenge, a retiree can establish a new routine that incorporates activities they enjoy. Engaging in physical exercise, pursuing hobbies, or enrolling in classes or workshops can provide structure and a sense of purpose. Setting goals and creating a daily schedule can help the retiree maintain a sense of usefulness and wellbeing.

Health and Wellbeing

As individuals age beyond retirement, health considerations become increasingly important. Retirement can bring about lifestyle changes that will impact on physical and mental wellbeing. Without the structure and demands of the workplace, retirees may find it somewhat challenging to maintain a healthy lifestyle and may even experience a loss of motivation to prioritize their health care, such as forgetting to take medication etc.

Retirees must prioritize their health by maintaining regular medical check-ups, engaging in physical exercise, and adopting healthy eating habits. Establishing a routine that incorporates these elements can contribute to overall wellbeing and a more enjoyable higher quality of life during retirement.

Retirement presents a mix of challenges and opportunities to which one needs to rapidly adjust in order to navigate this significant life transition. Addressing the loss of work identity, managing finances, adapting to social changes, establishing new routines, and prioritizing health are crucial components of adjusting to retirement.

By proactively addressing these challenges, retirees can transform them into opportunities for personal growth and fulfilment. Embracing one's newfound freedom, pursuing one's passions, engaging in meaningful and interesting activities, and fostering new social connections can contribute to a rewarding retirement experience. Remember, adjusting to retirement is a unique journey for each individual. Seeking support from loved ones, connecting with retirement communities, and seeking professional guidance can provide valuable insights and assistance during this life changing time. Embrace the challenges, seize the opportunities, and embark on a truly fulfilling retirement journey.

Creating a Purposeful Retirement Plan

Retirement marks a significant transition in our lives, a time when we bid farewell to the workforce and embark on a new chapter filled with opportunities for personal growth, meaningful pursuits, and a sense of purpose. It's a phase where we have the freedom to shape our days the way we like according to our hopes, needs, passions and aspirations.

Here we will explore the importance of creating a purposeful retirement plan or vision, to help guide you on a journey to enjoy a really fulfilling post-work life.

Reflecting on Your Values and Priorities

In the approach to retirement, hopefully you took some time to reflect upon your core values, interests, and priorities. What truly matters to you? What activities bring you joy and a sense of fulfilment? Now is the time to consider how you can align your retirement expectations with these aspects of your life. Whether it's spending quality time with family, pursuing a lifelong passion, or making a positive impact on your community, identifying your values and priorities will serve as a compass for your retirement journey.

Setting Goals and Objectives

Creating a purposeful retirement vision requires setting clear achievable goals and objectives. What do you hope to achieve during this new phase of your life? Set both short-term and long-term goals that encompass various aspects such as health, personal growth, relationships, and leisure. For example, one might aim to learn a new language, volunteer for a cause dear to your heart, or maintain an active and healthy lifestyle by regularly exercising, running, walking, jogging or joining a gym. Well-defined goals will provide direction and motivation as you move forward.

Exploring New Horizons

Retirement offers unique opportunities to explore new horizons and delve into areas you may not have had time for during your working years. Consider pursuing new hobbies, interests, or even career paths you've always been curious about but never had the time to explore. Engaging in new activities can foster personal growth, expand your social network, and bring a renewed sense of purpose. Whether it's taking up painting, joining a book club, or learning a musical instrument, embrace the joy of discovery and the endless possibilities that lie ahead.

Engaging in Lifelong Learning

Retirement doesn't mean the end of learning; in fact, it presents an ideal time to continue expanding your knowledge and skills. Lifelong learning has numerous benefits, including mental stimulation, improved cognitive function, and a broader perspective on the world. Explore educational opportunities such as workshops, online courses, or local community programs. By continuously challenging yourself to acquire an abundance of new knowledge, you'll stay intellectually engaged and cognitively aware, building on your personal growth and wellbeing.

Giving Back to Society

Retirement provides an excellent opportunity to give something back to society and make a positive impact. Consider how you can contribute your skills, experience, and time to meaningful causes or organizations in or around your area. Volunteering not only benefits the community but also enhances your own sense of purpose and fulfilment. Whether it's mentoring young professionals, supporting local charities, or sharing your expertise with nonprofit organizations, your contribution can create a ripple effect of appreciation for the positive change you are making.

Cultivating Relationships and Connections

Retirement is an opportune time to nurture and strengthen relationships with loved ones and cultivate new connections. Prioritize spending quality time with family and friends, as these relationships provide a sense of belonging and support. Additionally, seek out social groups, clubs, or organizations that align with your interests. Engaging in social activities will foster a sense of community and opens doors to new friendships, ensuring a rich and fulfilling retirement experience.

Creating a purposeful retirement vision is about proactively shaping your post-work life to align with your values, aspirations, and desire for fulfilment and improved wellbeing. It involves reflecting on your priorities, setting achievable goals, exploring new horizons, engaging in lifelong learning, giving back to society, and fostering meaningful connections. By adhering to this process, you can craft a retirement journey that brings joy, purpose, and a deep sense of satisfaction. Remember, retirement is not just a destination; it's a continuous exploration of the limitless possibilities that lie ahead.

CHAPTER

4

**Identifying Personal
Procrastination Patterns**

Self-reflection and awareness techniques to avoid procrastination triggers

When attempting to unlock our personal growth in the current times we live in, it is easy to get caught up in a torrent of responsibilities and completely lose sight of our own wellbeing. However, honest self-reflection and awareness techniques offer a transformational way to reconnect with ourselves and cultivate personal growth. In this chapter, we will dive into the depths of these techniques, exploring what a profound impact they can have on our lives. So, take a moment to concentrate on yourself, as we set off on a journey of self-discovery.

Mindful Meditation

At the heart of self-reflection lies the practice of mindful meditation. Find a quiet and comfortable space, close your eyes, and focus your attention on the present moment in time. Allow your thoughts to come and go without judgment, gently returning from time to time to the awareness of your actual breathing. Through regular meditation, you will develop an ability to observe your own thoughts and emotions, thereby, gaining an insight into your inner landscape. This heightened self-awareness will lay the foundations for some profound personal improvement.

Journaling for Clarity

Writing has for a long time been accepted as a powerful tool for clear self-reflection. Start a practice of journaling for a few minutes every day, by putting pen to paper and noting down your innermost thoughts and experiences. Begin by free-writing, allowing your thoughts to flow without censorship. As you dig deeper, reflect on your emotions, your challenges, and your successes. This concept will provide some clarity, allowing you to identify any patterns, discover any hidden motivations, and gain a fresh perspective on how you are progressing.

Seeking Feedback

Self-reflection need not be a solitary exercise because seeking some unbiased feedback from trusted family members, friends, or mentors can offer very valuable insights into any blind spots you may have and areas for improvement. Actively listen to their perspectives, without becoming defensive will serve you well.

Honest and unbiased feedback will serve as a mirror, allowing you to see yourself with more clarity and enabling you to make better informed choices for personal improvement.

Accepting Discomfort

Self-reflection often requires stepping outside one's comfort zone which can be uncomfortable at times. The discomfort that arises when examining your beliefs, values, and behaviors can actually turn into a valuable realisation that maybe some changes could be required. Question your assumptions and challenge any long-held ideas. This process will help to encourage personal improvement by fostering some adaptability and expanding your view of the world. Remember, growth mostly occurs outside the confines of familiarity.

Practicing Gratitude

Gratitude is a powerful catalyst for self-reflection and personal change. Take a moment each day to reflect on what you are grateful for. It could be something as simple as a kind gesture from a stranger or a moment of peace in a noisy situation. Cultivating gratitude moves your focus from what is lacking in your world to what is in abundance in your life, helping toward a more positive mindset and a better understanding of yourself.

Engaging in Self-Compassion

Self-reflection can sometimes reveal uncomfortable truths or mistakes from the past. In these moments, it is important to cultivate some self-compassion. Treat yourself with some kindness and understanding, acknowledging that growth and improvement is a lifelong journey filled with many ups and downs. Appreciate and use your imperfections as stepping stones toward personal improvement. Self-compassion will allow you to learn from your experiences without wallowing in destructive self-criticism.

Self-reflection and awareness techniques hold the key to unlocking one's inner potential and facilitating personal growth and improvement. By incorporating mindful meditation, journaling, seeking feedback, embracing discomfort, practicing gratitude, and cultivating self-compassion, we embark on a transformational journey toward self-discovery. Remember, self-reflection is not a one-time event but a lifelong practice that deepens our understanding of ourselves and enhances our relationships with others. Embrace this journey with openness and curiosity, and watch as it unfolds new dimensions of self-awareness and personal growth in your life.

Common Procrastination Triggers

Retirement is often seen as a time of leisure and freedom, where individuals can finally pursue their passions and enjoy a well-deserved break from the hum drum demands of work. However, many retirees will find themselves falling into the debilitating habit of procrastination, delaying urgent tasks and putting off important projects. In this chapter, we will explore some common procrastination triggers in retirement and discuss effective ways to overcome them.

Lack of Structure and Routine

One of the main reasons retirees succumb to procrastination is the sudden absence of a structured schedule. After years of sticking to strict work hours and deadlines, the newfound freedom of retirement can be overwhelming. Without a clear routine, it becomes easier to put off tasks and lose track of time.

Solution: Establishing a daily routine can provide structure and purpose to retirement life. Setting specific times for different activities, such as exercise, hobbies, and household chores, will help to maintain a sense of discipline and productive ability.

Ambiguous Goals and Lack of Direction

Retirement often brings a shift in priorities, and individuals may struggle to define meaningful goals and aspirations. Without clear objectives, it becomes easier to procrastinate, as there is no sense of urgency or purpose driving one's actions.

Taking the time to reflect on one's personal values and interests can help a retiree to identify new goals and projects. Whether it's learning a new skill, starting a new hobby, or volunteering, having a sense of purpose provides the motivation needed to overcome procrastination. Setting specific, achievable goals and breaking them down into smaller tasks can also make them more manageable and less daunting.

Fear of Failure or Perfectionism

Retirement can sometimes trigger a fear of failure or a desire for perfection. After years of striving for success in the workplace, individuals may hesitate to engage in new activities or pursue their passions, fearing they may not meet their own high standards or expectations.

Embracing a growth mindset is crucial in overcoming the fear of failure or lack of perfection. Realize that retirement is a time for personal growth and experimentation. It's okay to make mistakes and learn along the way.

Focus on the process rather than the outcome, and celebrate every small achievement. Seek support from one's peers or join groups where others are also exploring new endeavors, fostering a sense of camaraderie and shared experiences.

Proximity to Distractions

Retirement often coincides with increased access to distractions, such as television, social media, and other forms of entertainment. These distractions can easily use up valuable time and divert attention away from important tasks.

Solution: Create a dedicated workspace or a quiet area free from distractions where you can focus on specific tasks. Set up a time management technique, such as the Pomodoro Technique, which involves working in short bursts followed by short breaks, to maintain focus and productivity. Limit the use of electronic devices, tablets, cell phones etc., during your designated work periods to avoid falling into the mistake of mindless scrolling.

Loss of Accountability and External Deadlines

In retirement, the absence of colleagues, supervisors, and external deadlines can diminish the sense of accountability. Without the pressure to meet others' expectations, it becomes easier to delay tasks or abandon projects altogether.

Solution: Establishing self-accountability measures can help overcome this hurdle. Share your goals and aspirations with trusted friends or family members who can provide support and maybe even hold you accountable. Consider joining clubs or groups related to your interests, where you can find like-minded individuals who share similar goals. Collaborating with others on projects or setting self-imposed deadlines can provide the necessary structure and motivation to stay on track.

Retirement is a phase of life that should be cherished and enjoyed to the fullest extent. By recognizing the most common procrastination triggers and taking steps to implement effective strategies, a retiree can overcome the temptation to delay important tasks and make the most of their newfound freedom. Establishing structure, setting clear but achievable goals, embracing thoughts of improvement, minimizing distractions, and fostering accountability are essential steps toward a fulfilling and productive life in retirement. With a proactive approach, you can unlock your potential, embark on new adventures, and make your retirement years truly meaningful.

CHAPTER

5

Setting meaningful goals

Smart goal setting to align goals with personal values and interests

Retirement marks a significant milestone in one's life, offering an opportunity to embark on new adventures, pursue long-awaited dreams, and find fulfilment. However, to make the most of this chapter, retirees need to engage in smart goal setting. While retirement may signify a break from traditional work, setting meaningful objectives helps individuals stay motivated, maintain a sense of purpose, and enhance their overall well-being. In this article, we will delve into the importance of smart goal setting for retirees and provide practical tips on how to create and achieve goals during this exciting phase of life.

Why Smart Goal Setting Matters

Smart goal setting provides a framework for retirees to plan, organize, and prioritize their activities. By setting specific, measurable, achievable, relevant, and time-bound goals, retirees can harness their newfound freedom to enrich their lives in a purposeful manner. Here's why smart goal setting is vital for retirees:

Maintaining a sense of purpose: After years of dedicated work, retirement can sometimes leave individuals feeling a void in their lives. By setting goals, retirees can establish a renewed sense of purpose, ensuring they wake up each day with enthusiasm and determination.

Enhancing overall well-being: Engaging in activities that align with personal goals promotes mental, emotional, and physical well-being. Smart goal setting allows retirees to focus on self-improvement, fostering a sense of accomplishment and contentment.

Making the most of free time: Retirement offers an abundance of free time. Setting goals ensures retirees utilize this precious resource efficiently, avoiding stagnation and boredom. By pursuing meaningful objectives, retirees can stay engaged and continue personal growth.

Practical Tips for Smart Goal Setting

Reflect on personal values and passions: Begin the goal-setting process by reflecting on what truly matters to you. Consider the activities, hobbies, or causes that ignite your passion and align with your core values. This reflection will help guide you in identifying meaningful goals that resonate deeply with your interests.

Set specific and measurable goals: Vague goals are often challenging to achieve. Instead, aim for specific and measurable objectives. For example, rather than setting a goal to "travel more," define it as "visit three new countries within the next two years." Such clarity provides a clear target and enables you to track your progress effectively.

Prioritize and break down goals: Retirees often have an array of aspirations, and it can be overwhelming to tackle them all simultaneously. Prioritize your goals based on their importance and feasibility. Break larger goals into smaller, manageable tasks or milestones, making them less daunting and easier to accomplish.

Be realistic and flexible: While it's essential to challenge yourself, it's equally important to be realistic about your capabilities and limitations. Set goals that are attainable yet stretch you outside your comfort zone. Be open to adjusting your goals as circumstances change, allowing flexibility while staying focused on the desired outcomes.

Seek new experiences and learning opportunities: Retirement is an ideal time to explore new interests, hobbies, or skills. Consider setting goals that involve learning something new, such as playing a musical instrument, mastering a foreign language, or taking up painting. Embrace the opportunity to broaden your horizons and engage in lifelong learning.

Embrace health and well-being goals

Prioritizing health and well-being becomes even more crucial during retirement. Set goals related to physical fitness, such as maintaining a regular exercise routine, adopting a balanced diet, or participating in a sport or activity that you enjoy. Additionally, incorporate mental and emotional well-being goals, such as practicing meditation, joining a book club, or volunteering for a cause that resonates with you.

Track progress and celebrate achievements: Keep track of your progress towards your goals. Regularly assess your achievements, make necessary adjustments, and celebrate milestones along the way. Celebrating small victories provides a sense of accomplishment, maintaining motivation and fuelling your drive to pursue further goals.

Retirement is an exciting chapter in life, offering a multitude of opportunities to explore, grow, and find fulfilment. Smart goal setting empowers retirees to make the most of this precious phase, allowing them to maintain a sense of purpose, enhance overall well-being, and maximize their free time. By reflecting on personal values, setting specific and measurable goals, and embracing new experiences, retirees can embark on a journey of self-discovery and achievement. Remember, retirement is not just a destination; it's a chance to create an enriching and purposeful life beyond the traditional workplace. So, take the time to set smart goals and relish the joy and fulfilment they bring to your golden years.

Aligning Goals with Personal Values and Interests

Self-Reflection: Engage in introspection to identify your core values and interests. Consider your life experiences, the activities that energize you, and the values you hold dear. Write them down and gain clarity on what truly drives and inspires you.

Goal Evaluation: Assess your current goals and aspirations. Determine whether they align with your personal values and interests. Are there any goals that seem incongruent or disconnected from what truly matters to you? Reevaluate and refine your goals accordingly.

Define Meaningful Objectives: Based on your core values and interests, set specific, measurable, attainable, relevant, and time-bound (SMART) goals. Ensure that these goals resonate with your authentic self and reflect your passions. For example, if you value personal growth and have an interest in mindfulness, setting a goal to complete a meditation course can be both meaningful and aligned.

Prioritize and Focus

It's essential to prioritize your goals to avoid spreading yourself too thin. Determine which goals are most significant to you and focus your energy and resources on them. By concentrating on a few key goals, you increase your chances of success and fulfilment.

Take Action: Transform your goals into actionable steps. Break them down into smaller milestones and create a roadmap for achieving them. Maintain a sense of commitment, discipline, and resilience as you work towards aligning your actions with your values and interests.

Re-evaluate and Adapt

Life is a dynamic journey, and our values and interests may evolve over time. Regularly reassess your goals and ensure they continue to resonate with who you are becoming. Adjust and adapt your aspirations as needed to stay aligned with your personal growth.

Aligning our goals with our personal values and interests is a transformative process that can lead to a life filled with meaning, satisfaction, and fulfilment. By understanding our core values, exploring our passions, and setting purposeful goals, we embark on a journey that aligns our actions with our authentic selves. Remember, this is an ongoing process that requires self-reflection, adaptation, and perseverance. As you strive for alignment, you will discover that true success lies not only in achieving goals but in living a life that is deeply rooted in what truly matters to you.

CHAPTER

6

Developing effective Time Management Strategies

Retirement marks a significant transition in our lives, offering a newfound freedom and the opportunity to create a daily schedule that aligns with our desires and aspirations. While retirement may evoke images of lazy afternoons and spontaneous adventures, having a structured routine can enhance our well-being, productivity, and overall satisfaction during this phase. In this chapter, we'll explore the art of creating a retirement daily schedule that balances leisure, personal growth, and meaningful engagements.

Rise & Shine: Start Your Day with Purpose

Just because you're retired doesn't mean you need to abandon the concept of mornings. Establishing a consistent wake-up time can provide a sense of structure and purpose. Begin your day with a calming ritual, such as meditation or enjoying a cup of coffee while reading the news. Starting your morning mindfully can set a positive tone for the rest of the day.

Prioritize Your Physical Well-being

Physical fitness is a cornerstone of a healthy retirement. Incorporating regular exercise into your daily routine promotes cardiovascular health, strength, and mental clarity. Engage in activities that suit your preferences, whether it's walking, cycling, swimming, or practicing yoga. Consult a healthcare professional to determine the exercise regime that best suits your abilities and goals.

Pursue Personal Passions and Hobbies

Retirement presents an ideal opportunity to indulge in your passions and explore new interests. Dedicate a portion of your day to activities that bring you joy and satisfaction. This could include painting, gardening, playing a musical instrument, writing, or engaging in a creative pursuit you've always wanted to try but never got round to actually doing. Nurturing some personal hobbies can provide a sense of purpose and accomplishment.

Lifelong Learning - Expand Your Knowledge

Retirement is an excellent time to embark on a journey of continuous learning. Enrol in courses, attend workshops, or participate in seminars that align with your interests. Expanding your knowledge base not only stimulates your mind but also keeps you engaged and intellectually sharp. Take the opportunity to learn something new and stay curious.

Stay Socially Engaged - Foster Meaningful Connections

Maintaining social connections is essential for a fulfilling retirement. Dedicate some time to nurture relationships with family, friends, and your community. Join clubs or organizations that cater to your interests, participate in group activities, or volunteer for a cause you feel passionate about. Engaging with others can bring companionship, a sense of belonging, and an opportunity for personal growth.

Take Time for Relaxation and Reflection

Retirement is also about self-care and taking moments of relaxation and reflection. Incorporate periods of rest into your daily schedule. Read a book, enjoy a soothing shower or bath, or practice mindfulness exercises to promote inner peace and tranquility. By intentionally setting aside time for self-reflection, you can cultivate a deeper understanding of yourself and your aspirations during this chapter of life.

Engage with Nature and the Outdoors

Immerse yourself in the beauty of nature and the great outdoors. Plan regular outings to parks, gardens, or nature reserves. Engaging with the natural world not only provides physical exercise but also fosters a sense of peace and rejuvenation. Whether it's a leisurely stroll or an adventurous hike, spend time outdoors and enjoy its therapeutic benefits.

Evening Rituals - Unwind and Recharge

As the day comes to a close, establish some evening rituals that promote relaxation and restful sleep. Engage in activities that help you wind down, such as reading, listening to calming music, or practicing gentle stretching exercises. Create a peaceful environment in your bedroom to facilitate a good restive night's sleep, ensuring you wake up refreshed and ready to challenge the following day.

Crafting a well-structured retirement daily schedule allows you to make the most of this remarkable time in your life. Balancing personal pursuits, social engagements, physical activity, and relaxation can bring a sense of purpose, fulfilment, and joy to your retirement years. By following, and keeping to a daily routine, you'll find that retirement offers an abundance of opportunities for personal growth, meaningful connections, and the freedom to explore your passions. So, take the reins of your retirement and design a daily schedule that nourishes your mind, body, and spirit. Your golden years await!

Time Blocking and Prioritization Strategies

Unlocking the secrets to productivity in the hustle and bustle of our fast-paced lives, finding ways to stay organized and focused is crucial. Time blocking and prioritization strategies offer a powerful solution to the challenges of managing our ever-growing to-do lists, Let's look at these techniques and how they can help us optimize our time and accomplish more in our daily lives.

The Benefit of Time Blocking

At its core, time blocking is a method of scheduling specific time slots for different activities or tasks. By setting aside dedicated periods for focused tasks, social meetings, and even breaks, we can effectively structure our day and enhance our productivity.

One of the primary benefits of time blocking is that it promotes deep work—a state of intense concentration that allows us to tackle complex tasks and make significant progress. By designating uninterrupted time for specific activities, we create an environment that supports focused attention, enabling us to produce higher-quality work.

To implement time blocking effectively, start by dividing your day into discrete chunks. Assign each block to a specific task or activity, ensuring that it aligns with your goals and priorities. Whether it's working on a project, responding to emails, or engaging in creative brainstorming, allocating dedicated time slots will help you make steady progress and avoid distractions.

The Art of Prioritization

While time blocking helps structure our day, prioritization ensures that we invest our time and energy into the most important tasks. Prioritization is about identifying what matters most and allocating resources accordingly.

To effectively prioritize, it's essential to have a clear understanding of your goals and objectives. Take the time to assess the urgency and importance of each task. Urgent tasks demand immediate attention due to time sensitivity, while important tasks contribute significantly to long-term goals and overall success.

To aid in prioritization, consider using frameworks such as the Eisenhower Matrix. This matrix categorizes tasks based on their urgency and importance, allowing you to determine which tasks require immediate action, which can be delegated, and which should be eliminated.

By aligning your time blocks with high-priority tasks, you ensure that you make progress on what truly matters. This focused approach minimizes the risk of getting caught up in less impactful activities and helps you achieve meaningful results.

Benefits of Time Blocking and Prioritization

Adopting time blocking and prioritization strategies can yield a multitude of benefits in both personal and professional domains:

Enhanced Focus

By dedicating specific time blocks to particular tasks, you create a structured environment that promotes deep focus and concentration. This minimizes distractions and improves the quality of your work.

Increased Productivity

When you allocate time deliberately and prioritize tasks effectively, you optimize your productivity. You can accomplish more in less time and experience a sense of accomplishment.

Reduced Procrastination: Procrastination often stems from feeling overwhelmed by the sheer volume of tasks. Time blocking and prioritization break down complex tasks into manageable portions, reducing the tendency to procrastinate.

Better Work-Life Balance

These strategies help you strike a balance between work and personal life by ensuring that you allocate time for both. By setting aside dedicated blocks for relaxation and rejuvenation, you can prevent burnout and maintain overall well-being.

Improved Time Management

Time blocking and prioritization require thoughtful planning and organization. As you become more adept at these techniques, you develop a stronger sense of time management, allowing you to make the most of your available hours.

Tips for Effective Time Blocking & Prioritization

To make the most of time blocking and prioritization, consider the following tips:

Start with a Clear Plan

Begin each day or week with a clear plan of what needs to be accomplished. List your tasks, identify priorities, and allocate time blocks accordingly.

Be Realistic

Avoid overcommitting yourself by setting realistic expectations for each time block. Consider the estimated time required for each task and allocate buffer time for unforeseen circumstances.

Build in Flexibility

While time blocking aims to structure your day, it's essential to allow for flexibility. Unexpected events or urgent tasks may arise, requiring adjustments to your schedule. Be prepared to adapt when necessary.

Eliminate Distractions

During time blocks, create an environment conducive to focused work. Minimize distractions by turning off notifications, closing irrelevant tabs, and finding a quiet space to work.

Evaluate and Refine

Regularly assess the effectiveness of your time blocking and prioritization methods. Identify areas for improvement and refine your approach to optimize your productivity continually.

Summary

Time blocking and prioritization strategies empower us to take control of our time and accomplish more in our daily lives. By allocating specific time slots to tasks, we enhance our focus and minimize distractions. Simultaneously, prioritization ensures that we invest our time in activities that align with our goals and objectives.

While these strategies require discipline and planning, their benefits are significant. Enhanced productivity, reduced procrastination, and improved work-life balance are just a few of the rewards that come with implementing time blocking and prioritization in our lives.

So, embrace these techniques and unlock the power of productivity. Take charge of your time, make deliberate choices, and witness the transformative impact on your personal and professional endeavors.

CHAPTER

7

Overcoming Procrastination

In the vast realm of responsibilities and goals, it's not uncommon to feel overwhelmed by the sheer magnitude of tasks before us. However, there is a simple yet effective strategy that can transform even the most daunting undertaking into manageable and achievable milestones by breaking tasks into smaller steps. By dividing complex endeavors into bite-sized portions, we unlock a path to productivity and success that is both practical and attainable.

Understanding the Burden of Overwhelming Tasks

We've all experienced that sinking feeling when faced with a colossal task. The weight of it can be paralyzing, leaving us unsure of where to start or how to proceed. Breaking tasks into smaller steps allows us to overcome this hurdle by reducing the perceived enormity of the undertaking. It provides a clear roadmap and helps us focus on one achievable portion at a time.

Breaking Down Complexity

Task complexity can often be a significant roadblock to progress. By applying the principle of chunking, we can simplify intricate tasks into manageable subtasks. This process involves breaking down a task into smaller, distinct components that are easier to understand, execute, and track. As we conquer each subtask, we gain momentum and build confidence, propelling us forward towards the ultimate goal.

Improving Focus and Minimizing Distractions

Breaking tasks into smaller steps not only aids in task comprehension but also enhances our ability to maintain focus. By narrowing our attention to a single step, we minimize distractions and increase concentration. This focused approach fosters greater efficiency and productivity, as we direct our energy and resources towards specific, achievable objectives.

Overcoming Procrastination and Building Motivation

Procrastination is a common foe that can hinder progress and impede success. Breaking tasks into smaller steps provides a potent antidote to this procrastination trap. By setting achievable mini-goals, we create a sense of accomplishment with each completed step. This sense of progress fuels our motivation and propels us towards the next milestone. As we build momentum, we gain a renewed sense of purpose and determination.

Harnessing the Power of Planning and Organization

Breaking tasks into smaller steps necessitates careful planning and organization. This process allows us to chart our course and establish a clear roadmap for success. By delineating each step, we can allocate resources, set realistic timelines, and identify potential obstacles in advance. A well-structured plan provides a sense of direction and control, increasing our chances of achieving our desired outcome.

Inherent within the strategy of breaking tasks into smaller steps lies an iterative process. As we progress through each mini-task, we gain insights, refine our approach, and adapt our strategies accordingly. This iterative nature allows for continuous improvement, enabling us to optimize our efforts and maximize our outcomes. Small steps provide opportunities for reflection, course correction, and learning, fostering personal and professional growth.

In the realm of productivity and success, breaking tasks into smaller steps emerges as a vital and effective strategy. By fragmenting overwhelming endeavors into manageable chunks, we alleviate stress, enhance focus, and conquer procrastination. The power of planning, organization, and iterative refinement further solidifies the impact of this approach, enabling us to navigate complex tasks with greater efficiency and effectiveness.

Remember, each journey begins with a single step. By embracing the philosophy of breaking tasks into smaller steps, we unlock our potential for accomplishment and propel ourselves towards success. So, take that first step, savor the satisfaction of progress, and embrace the transformative power of breaking tasks into smaller, achievable milestones.

Implementing the Two Minute Rule

Procrastination, the nemesis of productivity, can plague even the most disciplined among us. The tendency to delay important tasks, whether due to fear, overwhelm, or a lack of motivation, hampers our progress. In the battle against this formidable foe, a technique called the Two Minute Rule has emerged as a powerful strategy. This method, when implemented with precision and intention, can help us overcome procrastination and unlock our full potential. In this article, we will delve into the depths of the Two Minute Rule and explore how it can be effectively employed to combat procrastination.

Understanding the Two Minute Rule

The Two Minute Rule is deceptively simple but incredibly effective. It centers around the idea that any task that can be completed in two minutes or less should be done immediately, without delay. This approach aims to eliminate the common tendency to put off small tasks, which can accumulate and create a sense of overwhelm over time. By addressing these short tasks promptly, we create momentum and a sense of accomplishment that propels us forward.

The Psychology Behind the Rule

At the heart of the Two Minute Rule lies the concept of activation energy. Activation energy refers to the mental effort required to start a task. For many individuals, the mere thought of initiating a task, regardless of its size or complexity, can be overwhelming. The Two Minute Rule helps to mitigate this challenge by lowering the activation energy. By committing to just two minutes, the mind perceives the task as less daunting, making it easier to begin.

The Ripple Effect of Starting

One of the remarkable aspects of the Two Minute Rule is its tendency to create a ripple effect. The act of starting a task, even for a brief period, often leads to an increased likelihood of continuing beyond the initial two minutes. Once we overcome the inertia of inaction, we tap into a wellspring of motivation and find ourselves engaged in the task for longer durations. The psychological barrier of starting is often more significant than the actual work involved, and the Two Minute Rule effectively dismantles this barrier.

Applying the Two Minute Rule

To implement the Two Minute Rule effectively, it is crucial to develop a systematic approach. Here are some practical steps to consider:

Identify tasks suitable for the Two Minute Rule: Scan your to-do list and pinpoint tasks that can be completed in two minutes or less. These may include responding to emails, making phone calls, organizing files, or tidying your workspace.

Prioritize and sequence: Determine the order in which you will tackle these short tasks. Consider any dependencies or time-sensitive elements that might influence the sequence. By creating a logical progression, you ensure a smooth flow of productivity.

Set a timer: Dedicate two minutes of focused effort to each task. Set a timer to maintain a sense of urgency and prevent distractions from derailing your progress. Avoid the temptation to extend the time for any particular task, as this might compromise the efficiency of the approach.

Celebrate completion:

Acknowledge and appreciate the completion of each task, no matter how small. Celebrating these victories reinforces a positive mindset and further fuels your motivation to continue.

Evaluate and adapt

Regularly assess the effectiveness of the Two Minute Rule in your workflow. Observe how it influences your productivity and make adjustments as needed. Not every task will fit within the two-minute timeframe, so be mindful of when to apply this rule and when to allocate more substantial blocks of time.

In the eternal battle against procrastination, the Two Minute Rule stands as a stalwart ally. By addressing short tasks promptly and consistently, we develop a habit of action that propels us forward. The psychological power of starting, even for a mere two minutes, cannot be understated. With each small victory, we build momentum, overcome inertia, and conquer procrastination's grip on our lives.As you set off on your journey to implement the Two Minute Rule, remember to approach it with intention and precision. Identify suitable tasks, establish a sequence, set a timer, and celebrate your progress. Embrace the power of this deceptively simple strategy and watch as your productivity soars, leaving procrastination in its wake. The Two Minute Rule is a testament to the profound impact that small actions can have on our lives. Seize the opportunity to overcome procrastination, one two-minute interval at a time, and unlock your true potential.

CHAPTER

8

Nurturing Focus and Concentration

In today's fast-paced and technology-driven world, maintaining focus has become a challenge of epic proportions. Our attention is constantly pulled in multiple directions, leaving us feeling overwhelmed and scattered. However, amidst this chaos, there is a proven and ancient solution that can help us regain control of our wandering minds: mindfulness and meditation.

Understanding Mindfulness

At its essence, mindfulness is the practice of intentionally directing our attention to the present moment. It involves observing our thoughts, feelings, and bodily sensations without judgment. By cultivating a state of non-reactive awareness, we can disengage from distractions and bring our full attention to the task at hand.

The Power of Meditation

Meditation serves as the vehicle through which we develop mindfulness. It is a systematic practice that involves training the mind to focus and redirect our thoughts. Through meditation, we cultivate mental clarity, emotional stability, and resilience. It provides a sanctuary of stillness amidst the chaos of our daily lives, allowing us to tap into our inner resources and optimize our cognitive abilities.

Calming the Mental Storm

Our minds are often filled with a whirlwind of thoughts, worries, and external stimuli that pull us away from the present moment. Mindfulness and meditation act as an anchor, enabling us to calm the storm within. By observing our thoughts without getting caught up in them, we can reduce mental clutter and create a more conducive environment for sustained focus.

Strengthening Cognitive Control

Mindfulness and meditation have been shown to enhance our cognitive control, which refers to the ability to maintain focus, inhibit distractions, and switch between tasks. By training our minds to remain centered on a chosen point of focus, such as the breath or a specific sensation, we develop the capacity to regulate our attention more effectively in daily life.

Heightening Self-Awareness

Self-awareness is a fundamental aspect of mindfulness. Through regular meditation practice, we become intimately acquainted with our own mental patterns, including tendencies towards distraction and mind-wandering. This heightened self-awareness allows us to recognize when our focus is slipping and gently guide it back to the present moment, enhancing our ability to sustain attention.

Cultivating Resilience

One of the most valuable benefits of mindfulness and meditation is the cultivation of resilience. By training our minds to remain calm and non-reactive in the face of distractions, stress, and challenges, we become more resilient in our ability to bounce back and refocus. This mental fortitude allows us to navigate the inevitable ups and downs of life with greater composure and clarity.

In a world where our attention is constantly divided, mindfulness and meditation offer a sanctuary of focus and clarity. By engaging in these practices, we can develop the ability to sustain our attention, regulate our mental processes, and navigate the demands of modern life with greater ease. So, let us embark on this journey of self-discovery and cultivate the power of mindfulness and meditation to unlock our full potential for improved focus and mental well-being.

How to Stay Focused (and Sane) in a Chaotic World by battling distractions

Life can sometimes feel like a circus, with distractions and interruptions performing an acrobatic routine to throw us off balance. In this high-tech, fast-paced era, maintaining focus has become a precious art form. But fear not, fellow humans, for I bring you a guide to reducing distractions and interruptions. Prepare yourself for a slightly amusing but seriously effective journey toward Zen-like concentration!

The 'Doomscrolling' Detox

Let's start with a common modern ailment - doomscrolling. We've all been there, scrolling through an endless morass of news, memes, and cat videos. It's time to break the cycle! Allocate specific periods for digital detoxes and limit your social media binges. Disconnect from the virtual world and get with the reality around you. Trust me, the outside world still exists.

The Email Abyss

Oh dear, emails—the never-ending vortex of our professional lives. Taming this beast requires discipline and strategy. Instead of obsessively checking your inbox every five minutes, set designated times to tackle your emails. And remember, the world won't crumble if you don't reply within milliseconds. Train yourself to prioritize and filter your messages, ensuring only the most important ones steal your attention.

Sneaky, unwanted, annoying Notifications

The sweet seduction of notifications! They beckon with their alluring vibrations and intrusive chirping. But fear not, for there's a way to tame these digital annoyances. Silence them! Mute non-essential notifications and let your phone or computer rest in peace. Allow yourself to focus on the task at hand without being distracted by every ping, ding, or ring. Your concentration will thank you.

The Art of Setting Boundaries

We're all guilty of being too nice sometimes, and that can lead to interruptions galore. Set clear boundaries and communicate them with your loved ones, coworkers, and even pets (though they might not fully grasp the concept). Establishing quiet hours or specific periods for uninterrupted work will send a message that you mean business. Respect your boundaries, and others will follow suit.

The Multitasking Myth

The great multitasking myth. We've all tried juggling a million tasks simultaneously, convinced we're productivity wizards. Spoiler alert: we're not. Research shows that multitasking actually diminishes focus and productivity. So, instead of attempting to perform a symphony of tasks, focus on one at a time. Give each task the attention it deserves, and you'll accomplish more with less stress.

The Allure of Procrastination

Procrastination is a formidable enemy of productivity. It disguises itself as relaxation, tempting us with Netflix marathons and online shopping sprees. But remember, dear reader, procrastination is a wily creature. Combat it with effective time management techniques, such as the Pomodoro Technique. Set a timer for 25 minutes of focused work, followed by a short break. Rinse and repeat. Before you know it, procrastination will be begging for mercy.

Reducing distractions and interruptions is an ongoing battle that requires consistent effort. By detoxing from doomscrolling, taming your inbox, muting notifications, setting boundaries, ditching multitasking, and defeating procrastination, you'll be well on your way to a more focused and productive life.

Remember, please, the art of reducing distractions is like learning to juggle flaming swords—it takes practice, determination, and maybe a few singed eyebrows. But fear not, for you are capable of achieving greatness. Embrace the power within you, and let the circus of distractions become a mere background noise in the grand symphony of your focused existence.

Now, go forth and conquer the world—one undistracted step at a time!

Mastering Focus

Strategies for Reducing Distractions and Interruptions in an increasingly fast-paced and interconnected world, staying focused has become a valuable skill. The ability to concentrate on important tasks without succumbing to distractions and interruptions is essential for productivity and overall well-being. In this section, we will explore effective strategies to reduce distractions and interruptions, allowing you to reclaim control over your attention and achieve your goals.

Create a Distraction-Free Environment

Your environment plays a significant role in your ability to focus. Minimize visual and auditory distractions by organizing your workspace. Clear clutter, ensure adequate lighting, and eliminate background noise when possible. Consider using noise-cancelling headphones or playing soothing music to create a calm atmosphere conducive to concentration.

Prioritize and Plan

Effective time management is key to reducing distractions. Begin each day by identifying your most important tasks and setting realistic goals. Prioritize your to-do list based on importance and urgency. Breaking down larger tasks into smaller, manageable steps can help prevent overwhelm and increase focus. By having a clear plan, you can maintain a sense of direction and purpose throughout the day.

Practice Single-Tasking

Multitasking may seem like a productive approach, but research suggests otherwise. Engaging in multiple tasks simultaneously divides your attention and reduces efficiency. Instead, embrace single-tasking. Focus on one task at a time, giving it your undivided attention until completion or a designated break. By immersing yourself fully in each task, you enhance productivity and the quality of your work.

Start Time Blocking

Time blocking is a powerful technique that involves scheduling specific blocks of time for focused work. Allocate uninterrupted periods for important tasks and guard these blocks fiercely. Communicate your availability to colleagues, friends, and family, establishing boundaries that respect your dedicated work periods. By proactively managing your time, you can minimize interruptions and optimize productivity.

Manage Digital Distractions

Our devices, while invaluable tools, can also be significant sources of distraction. Take control of your digital environment by managing notifications. Disable non-essential notifications or establish "do not disturb" settings during focused work periods. Consider using productivity apps or browser extensions that block access to distracting websites or limit your time on social media platforms.

Establish Clear Communication Channels

Effective communication is crucial in reducing interruptions. Establish clear guidelines with colleagues and family members regarding when and how interruptions are appropriate. Use communication tools such as email or instant messaging to minimize face-to-face interruptions. Encourage others to use these channels when possible, allowing you to manage your time and attention more effectively.

Practice Mindfulness

Mindfulness is a practice that cultivates awareness and presence in the present moment. By training your mind to stay focused on the task at hand, you become better equipped to recognize and redirect distractions. Engage in mindfulness exercises, such as deep breathing or meditation, to improve your ability to sustain attention and reduce the impact of external distractions.

Reducing distractions and interruptions is a continuous endeavor that requires conscious effort and discipline. By creating a distraction-free environment, prioritizing tasks, practicing single-tasking, utilizing time blocking, managing digital distractions, establishing clear communication channels, and incorporating mindfulness, you can significantly enhance your ability to focus.

Remember, maintaining focus is a skill that can be developed over time. Be patient with yourself as you implement these strategies and adapt them to your unique circumstances. With dedication and perseverance, you will gradually regain control over your attention, leading to increased productivity, improved well-being, and a greater sense of accomplishment in both your personal and social life.

CHAPTER

9

Building Motivation and Inspiration

Motivation is the driving force behind human behavior, pushing us to achieve our goals and reach new heights. While extrinsic motivation, such as rewards and recognition, can provide temporary bursts of energy, it is intrinsic motivation that holds the key to long-term success and personal fulfilment. Intrinsic motivation is the internal desire, passion, and curiosity that propels us to pursue activities for the sheer joy and satisfaction they bring. It is a powerful force that, when properly cultivated, can unlock our full potential and lead to sustained growth and achievement.

So, how can one cultivate intrinsic motivation? It begins with understanding the core elements that fuel this internal fire and creating an environment that nurtures its growth.

Firstly, autonomy plays a crucial role in fostering intrinsic motivation. When individuals have a sense of control over their actions and decisions, they feel empowered and motivated to pursue their interests with greater enthusiasm. This can be achieved by offering choices and opportunities for self-direction. Whether it's in the workplace, education, or personal endeavors, allowing individuals to have a say in their tasks, projects, and learning experiences helps foster a sense of ownership and fuels their intrinsic motivation.

Next, mastery and competence are vital factors that contribute to intrinsic motivation. As human beings, we naturally seek to develop and improve our skills. When we witness progress and see ourselves getting better at something, it ignites a sense of accomplishment and drives us to continue our efforts. To cultivate intrinsic motivation, it is essential to set clear and achievable goals, provide constructive feedback, and offer opportunities for growth and skill development. This fosters a growth mindset, where individuals view challenges as opportunities to learn and refine their abilities.

Another crucial aspect of cultivating intrinsic motivation is the presence of a meaningful purpose. When individuals understand the greater significance of their actions and how they contribute to a larger cause, they become more engaged and motivated.

Connecting tasks and activities to a purpose beyond personal gain instils a sense of meaning and fulfilment. Leaders, educators, and mentors can help individuals discover and align their personal values and passions with their work or pursuits, helping to fuel their vitally important motivation.

Moreover, fostering a supportive and positive environment is vital for cultivating this motivation. Humans thrive in environments where they feel safe, encouraged, and supported. Building relationships based on trust, empathy, and respect creates a foundation for individuals to flourish.

Recognizing and celebrating achievements, offering praise and encouragement, and providing emotional support during setbacks are all ways to foster intrinsic motivation. A positive environment instills a sense of belonging and confidence, empowering individuals to take risks, explore their interests, and persevere in the face of challenges.

Furthermore, cultivating intrinsic motivation requires fostering curiosity and a love for learning. The desire to explore new ideas, acquire knowledge, and expand our understanding of the world is a fundamental aspect of human nature. Encouraging individuals to ask questions, seek out information, and pursue intellectual curiosity nurtures intrinsic motivation. Creating opportunities for discovery, experimentation, and personal growth stimulates the mind and fuels a passion for learning that can last a lifetime.

Of course, it is important to note that cultivating said intrinsic motivation is an ongoing process that requires continuous effort and adaptation.

Different individuals are motivated by different factors, and what may ignite the flame of intrinsic motivation in one person might not do the same for another. As leaders, educators, and individuals ourselves, we must be attuned to the unique needs and aspirations of those around us. By observing, listening, and adapting our approaches, we can create environments and experiences that foster intrinsic motivation in others and within ourselves.

In conclusion, cultivating intrinsic motivation is a transformative journey that empowers individuals to unleash their full potential and find true fulfilment in their endeavors. Through autonomy, mastery, purpose, positive environments, curiosity, and a love for learning, we can create the fertile ground needed to nurture intrinsic motivation. As we embrace this powerful force within ourselves and those around us, we unlock the key to sustained growth, achievement, and a life well-lived. So, go to it and get started on this journey and inspire the world with your incredible intrinsic motivation.

Rewarding Progress and Celebrating Achievements

Nurturing growth and recognizing excellence in the pursuit of personal and professional development, progress and achievements serve as essential markers of growth and success. Recognizing and rewarding these milestones not only provide motivation and encouragement but also foster a culture of excellence. So, let us look into the significance of rewarding progress and celebrating achievements, highlighting the importance of acknowledging and honoring these remarkable moments.

The Power of Recognition

At the heart of rewarding progress and celebrating achievements lies the power of recognition. When we acknowledge the efforts and advancements made by individuals, teams, or organizations, we validate their hard work and dedication. Recognition acts as a catalyst, fueling the desire to continue striving for excellence and surpassing previous accomplishments. It creates a positive feedback loop, inspiring others to pursue their own goals and contribute to a collective success.

Motivation and Engagement

Rewarding progress and celebrating achievements serves as a powerful tool for motivation and engagement. When individuals are recognized for their progress, they feel a sense of value and appreciation. This recognition fuels their motivation further, driving them to persist and achieve even more.

By celebrating achievements, we reinforce a culture that values growth, effort, and perseverance. This, in turn, boosts engagement levels, leading to higher productivity and satisfaction among individuals and teams.

Fostering a Growth Mindset

Celebrating achievements goes hand in hand with cultivating a growth mindset. By recognizing progress, we emphasize the importance of continuous learning and improvement. When we celebrate achievements, we acknowledge not only the end result but also the process, effort, and resilience that led to success. This mindset shift encourages individuals to embrace challenges, view setbacks as opportunities for growth, and constantly seek ways to better develop their skills and abilities.

Building Confidence and Self-Efficacy

Rewarding progress and celebrating achievements has a profound impact on an individual's confidence and self-efficacy. When accomplishments are acknowledged, individuals develop a sense of belief in their own capabilities. This newfound confidence empowers them to take on new challenges and tackle more ambitious goals. By regularly rewarding progress, we provide individuals with the affirmation and validation they need to overcome self-doubt and reach their full potential.

Cultivating a Positive Culture

A culture that recognizes and celebrates achievements is one that fosters positivity, collaboration, and a sense of belonging. When accomplishments are shared and celebrated within a community or organization, it creates a supportive environment where individuals feel valued and appreciated. This positive culture not only enhances overall morale but also encourages teamwork, knowledge-sharing, and the pursuit of collective goals.

Recognizing progress and achievements reinforces the notion that success is a shared responsibility, driving individuals and teams to collaborate and achieve together.

Rewarding progress and celebrating achievements forms the backbone of a thriving and successful environment.

By recognizing and honoring the efforts, growth, and accomplishments of an individual or team, we encourage and foster motivation, engagement, and a culture of excellence. This recognition not only boosts confidence and self-efficiency but also cultivates a growth mindset that promotes continuous learning and improvement. Moreover, by celebrating achievement, we create a positive and supportive culture that encourages collaboration and shared success.

As we navigate our personal and professional journey, never underestimate the significance of rewarding progress and celebrating achievements. Together, let us nurture growth, recognize excellence, and build a future where every step forward is met with the applause and appreciation it truly deserves.

CHAPTER

10

Accountability and Support

In our quest for personal and professional growth, we often come across roadblocks and distractions which hinder our intended progress.

It can be challenging to stay focused, motivated, and accountable to ourselves, especially when faced with obstacles and temptations, but there is a powerful tool we have at our disposal which can help us to navigate these challenges and propel us toward success.

Accountability partners

An accountability partner is someone who shares our goals, values, and aspirations. They can act as a support system for us, by offering encouragement, guidance, and a gentle push when we need it most. This person can hold us responsible for our actions, ensuring that we stay on track and follow through with all, or most of our commitments.

The true value of an accountability partner lies in their ability to provide us with an external perspective on how we are doing in our journey. We often have blind spots and biases that can hinder our progress. Our accountability partner serves as a mirror, reflecting our actions and decisions back to us. They can help us to identify areas where we can improve, provide constructive feedback, by pushing and encouraging us to achieve a higher standard.

Accountability partners also serve as a source of motivation and inspiration. When we face challenges or feel overwhelmed, they are there to remind us of our goals and the reasons why we set out on this path in the first place. Their unwavering support and belief in our possible abilities can be a powerful catalyst for getting through the occasional difficult times.

Moreover, an accountability partner can help us establish and maintain a sense of discipline. They hold us accountable for our commitments, ensuring that we follow through with our intentions.

By having someone to answer to, we are less likely to find or make excuses, or worse, succumb to destructive procrastination.

This level of accountability creates a sense of urgency and can enhance our commitment to achieving the goals we have set.

Another key benefit of an accountability partner is the opportunity for mutual growth. Through open and honest communication, we can share our knowledge, experiences, and insights. This exchange of ideas can in turn, broaden both our perspectives, challenge our assumptions, and spark new possibilities.

Our accountability partner may have faced similar obstacles or achieved similar goals, thereby being in a better position to offer valuable advice and ideas for achieving our intended success.

In addition to providing guidance and motivation, accountability partners foster a sense of camaraderie and support. Knowing that we have someone in our corner, cheering us on and celebrating our victories, creates a sense of belonging and encouragement.

This kind of support can be a source of strength during challenging times and a reminder that we are not alone on our journey.

One of the often-overlooked aspects of accountability partnerships is the element of self-reflection they bring. Regular check-ins with our accountability partner can provide a very useful opportunity to assess our progress, evaluate our strategies, and make adjustments if and when necessary. This self-reflection can help us to learn from our successes and failures, allowing us to fine-tune our approach, and continue our improvement.

To make the most of an accountability partnership, it is crucial to establish clear goals and expectations from the outset. Both partners should have a shared understanding of what success looks like and the steps required to get there. Regular communication and check-ins are essential to track progress, address challenges, and celebrate milestones together.

It is also important to choose an accountability partner who is reliable, trustworthy, and committed to their own and your growth. Look for someone who shares your views and values, understands your ambitions, and has a genuine interest in seeing you succeed. The partnership should be built on mutual trust, respect, honesty, and a commitment to holding each other accountable.

While accountability partnerships offer numerous benefits, they are not a substitute for personal responsibility and self-discipline. Ultimately, we are accountable for our own actions and choices. Our accountability partner is there to guide and support us, but it is up to us to take ownership of our goals and targets, and put in the necessary effort to achieve them.

In conclusion, accountability partners are invaluable allies on our journey to success. They provide support, guidance, and motivation, while holding us accountable for our actions. Through regular check-ins, open communication, and shared experiences, accountability partners can help us stay focused, while navigating various challenges, and unlocking our true potential. So, if you're ready to take your goals to the next level, consider finding an accountability partner who can be a trusted companion on your path to the success you want.

Joining supportive retirement groups to improve well-being and connections in the golden years of retirement. Retirement marks a significant milestone in our lives, a time to say goodbye to the working world and start a new chapter in our life of freedom and self-discovery.

However, this sudden change from the normal working environment to the new-found freedom can sometimes lead to a feeling of isolation or a lack of purpose. That's where joining supportive retirement groups can make all the difference.

These communities offer a range of benefits, from fostering social connections to promoting overall well-being. In this respect, we'll look into the importance of joining such groups, and exploring the positive impact they can have on our lives during this new stage in our life.

Combating Social Isolation

Retirement frequently brings unusual changes in our social lives. Work colleagues who were once daily companions may drift apart as everyone follows their own retirement paths in different directions.

In this context, joining supportive retirement groups becomes very important in combating any social isolation. These communities or groups provide a nurturing environment where one can connect with like-minded peers who probably understand the unique challenges and experiences involved in retirement.

Sharing stories, engaging in interesting discussions, and taking part in group activities can help create a sense of belonging and often help to create new and maybe lasting friendships.

Stimulating Intellectual Engagement

Retirement doesn't mean the end of intellectual growth; in fact, it can be a time of renewed curiosity and exploration. Supportive retirement groups offer opportunities to engage in intellectually stimulating activities, such as book clubs, educational workshops, outings, or discussion forums.

Such groups can serve as a platform for sharing knowledge, exchanging ideas, and expanding one's horizons. By participating in such activities, a retiree can continue to learn, exercise their brain, and keep their cognitive abilities sharp.

Life is a varied journey filled with ups and downs, and retirement is no exception. Joining supportive retirement groups provides a safe space to share one's thoughts, concerns, and emotions. Being part of a community that understands and empathizes with the challenges retirees face can be immensely helpful and comforting.

Whether it's coping with health issues, adjusting to a new routine, or navigating changes in one's personal relationships, these groups offer a support network that can provide solace, guidance, and a listening ear.

Maintaining Physical and Mental Well-Being

Retirement groups often place a strong emphasis on health and well-being. Regular physical activities, such as walking groups, yoga classes, or swimming sessions, can help retirees maintain their physical fitness and overall health. Moreover, these groups often organize varied informational sessions on topics such as nutrition, mindfulness, and stress management, or promoting holistic well-being.

By prioritizing self-care and adopting healthy habits, a retiree can enjoy a fulfilling and vibrant retirement.

Engaging in Purposeful Activities

Retirement is a time to explore new passions, pursue long-held interests, or engage in meaningful activities that may have been put on hold during our working years. Supportive retirement groups offer a wealth of opportunities to get involved in community service, volunteer work, or advocacy initiatives. By contributing to a cause or helping others, a retiree can experience a renewed sense of purpose, fulfilment, and personal growth. These activities not only benefit the individual but also have a positive impact on society as a whole.

Retirement is a phase of life that should be cherished and enjoyed. Joining supportive retirement groups allows an individual to thrive in this new phase of their life by fostering previously unknown social connections, providing intellectual stimulation, offering emotional support, and promoting overall well-being. By actively participating in these communities, retirees can combat social isolation, maintain their mental and physical health, and discover a renewed sense of purpose. So, if you're on the threshold of retirement or have already embarked on this journey, consider the enriching benefits that supportive retirement groups can bring to your life.

Grab the opportunities that lie ahead, and make the most of your retirement years with the support and camaraderie of like-minded people.

CHAPTER

11

Managing Technology and Social Media

In the present age of abundant technology, we find ourselves surrounded by a digital landscape that demands our constant attention. The allure of social media, coupled with the ever-present stream of notifications and entertainment options, can easily lead us down a path of complete distraction and reduced productivity. However, it is always in our power to regain control over our digital distractions and find a sensible balance between the benefits of technology and the need for focused, meaningful engagement. In this chapter, we will dig into the importance of limiting digital distractions and explore some practical ideas for managing technology and social media in a more intentional manner.

Recognizing the Impact of Digital Overload

The first step in addressing digital distractions is to acknowledge their pervasive influence on our lives. Excessive use of technology and social media has been linked to diminishing attention spans, a reduction in productivity, and even an adverse effect on mental health. The constant availability of information, coupled with the addictive nature of social media, can badly disrupt our ability to concentrate, impede our ability to complete tasks efficiently, and negatively impact our overall well-being. By recognizing the potential harm that excessive digital engagement can cause, we can begin to take some proactive steps towards limiting its increasing hold over our lives.

Establishing Boundaries and Prioritizing Focus

One of the most effective ways to limit digital distractions is by establishing clear boundaries. Set specific periods during the day when you will dedicate yourself to focused work, or personal activities without the intrusion of technology. Consider creating a daily routine that sets out specific periods for checking emails and engaging with social media, while allocating dedicated time for more important tasks that require sustained attention. By setting clear boundaries, you will create an environment that allows for better concentration and reduces the temptation to constantly engage with your digital devices.

Using Productivity Tools and Applications

Technology, despite its potential to distract, can also offer solutions to the problem it creates. There are numerous productivity tools and applications readily available which can effectively help one to manage digital distractions. Time-tracking apps, for instance, enable you to monitor and regulate the time spent on various activities, allowing you to identify areas where excessive engagement occurs. Similarly, browser extensions and applications can block or limit access to distracting websites and social media platforms, providing a gentle reminder for you to stay focused on your intended tasks. By utilizing these tools, you can create a digital environment that supports your efforts to minimize any possible distractions while allowing you to maximize your productivity.

Practicing Mindfulness in Digital Consumption

In the midst of the constant barrage of information and content, it is vital to cultivate a sense of mindfulness in our digital consumption. Before mindlessly clicking on links or opening social media apps, pause for a moment and reflect on the purpose and value of your engagement. Ask yourself whether the activity aligns with your goals, whether it contributes positively to your well-being or learning, and whether it is really necessary in the present moment or will it keep until later. By consciously choosing what we delve into and for what purpose, we can start to filter out the noise and focus only on the digital content that truly enriches our lives.

Creating a Supportive Physical Environment

The physical environment in which we engage with technology can significantly impact our ability to limit distractions. Assign specific spaces in your home or workplace that are technology-free zones, allowing you to disconnect and find relief from the constant stream of unnecessary online stimuli. Additionally, organizing your physical workspace in a way that minimizes the presence of digital devices and promotes a sense of calm can greatly improve focus and reduce the temptation to engage in distracting online activities. By consciously designing a supportive physical environment, you create a space conducive to productivity and reducing digital interference.

Fostering Real-World Connections

While social media platforms offer a means of connecting with others, it is also important to balance virtual interactions with real-world connections. Cultivate relationships and engage in activities that allow for face-to-face communication and genuine human interaction. Prioritize quality time with loved ones, friends, neighbors, and trades people, take time to participate in hobbies that require offline engagement, and make an effort to disconnect from technology during social interactions. By building more real-world connections, we can regain a sense of fulfilment that goes beyond the temporary attraction of the digital world.

In our increasingly digital world, limiting distractions has become an important necessity for maintaining focus, productivity, and overall well-being. By recognizing the impact of digital overload, establishing boundaries, utilizing productivity tools, practicing mindfulness, creating supportive physical environments, and fostering real-world connections, we can reclaim control over our digital lives. It is through these intentional efforts that we can strike a harmonious balance between the benefits of technology and the need for focused, meaningful engagement, ultimately allowing us to thrive in both the digital and physical realms.

Utilizing Technology for Improved Productivity

Retirement marks a significant milestone in life, offering an opportunity for rest, relaxation, and the pursuit of personal interests. While the notion of retirement often conjures up images of a break from technology and digital distractions, the reality is that technology can be harnessed to enhance productivity even in this phase of life. By effectively managing technology and social media, retirees can leverage these tools to streamline tasks, stay connected, and explore new avenues of learning. Here, we will explore the ways in which technology can be employed to boost productivity during retirement.

Embracing Digital Organization

One of the key benefits of technology in retirement is its capacity to streamline organizational tasks. From digital calendars and to-do lists to note-taking apps, retirees can efficiently manage their schedules and prioritize activities. By embracing these digital tools, a retiree can enhance productivity by ensuring that important appointments and engagements are never overlooked, allowing for effective time management and reducing the risk of missed opportunities.

Apps for Leveraging Productivity

In the huge landscape of mobile applications, there are numerous tools designed specifically to aid and enhance productivity. A retirees can benefit from utilizing apps that facilitate good financial management, task tracking, and goal setting. With these tools, one can stay on top of one's financial obligations, set and monitor personal goals, and track progress toward achieving them. By harnessing the power of productivity apps, a retiree can maintain a sense of purpose and accomplishment throughout their retirement years.

Engaging in Lifelong Learning

Retirement is an ideal time to indulge in personal interests and engage in some lifelong learning. Technology offers easy access to a vast array of online resources, courses, and tutorials. Online learning platforms provide multiple opportunities to explore new subjects, acquire new skills, and delve deeper into existing passions. Through webinars, e-books, and educational websites, retirees can embark on intellectual pursuits, fostering personal growth and expanding their horizons.

Connecting Through Social Media

Social media platforms provide a vast array of opportunities for connection, community engagement, and sharing experiences with loved ones and others.

A retiree can use social media to stay connected with family and friends, fostering relationships regardless of physical distance. Moreover, social media can facilitate participation in interest-based groups and forums, enabling easy interaction with like-minded individuals, exchange of ideas, and finding support if needed. By harnessing the positive aspects of social media, a retiree can maintain social connections and establish new relationships, enhancing their overall well-being and sense of belonging.

Remote Collaboration and Volunteering

Technology has revolutionized the way we work, offering new opportunities for remote collaborations. Retirees who wish to engage in part-time work or volunteer activities can utilize technology to contribute their own expertise and skills from the comfort of their own home. Remote collaboration tools, video conferencing platforms, and project management software enable a retiree to engage in meaningful work, share their knowledge, and make a positive impact within their community, all while maintaining flexibility and a healthy work-life balance.

Retirement is a phase of life characterized by newfound freedom and the pursuit of personal fulfilment and happiness. In this digital age, technology can serve as a valuable ally in enhancing productivity during retirement. By effectively managing technology and social media, we can leverage these tools to streamline tasks, stay organized, and expand our horizons. By embracing digital organization, leveraging productivity apps, engaging in lifelong learning, connecting through social media, and exploring remote collaboration, we can navigate the digital landscape with confidence and utilize technology to its fullest potential. Through thoughtful and purposeful use of technology, retirees can enhance their productivity, maintain social connections, and embark on fulfilling endeavors, ensuring that their retirement years are accomplished, satisfying and enjoyable.

CHAPTER

12

Balancing Leisure and Productivity

Retirement is often hailed as the golden period of life, a time when we can finally say goodbye to the alarm clocks, deadlines, and the daily grind. It's an opportunity to savor the fruits of our labor and indulge in the activities we love. While financial planning and health considerations are essential for a successful retirement, let's not forget the important role of leisure. In this delightful area, we'll explore the importance of leisure in retirement, taking a light-hearted yet serious look at how embracing leisure can bring joy, fulfilment, and sanity to your golden years.

Unleash Your Inner Child

Remember the days of recess, playgrounds, and carefree laughter? Well, retirement offers a second chance to tap into that time of youthful spirit. Leisure activities not only bring joy but also stimulate the mind and body, keeping them sharp and engaged. Whether it's taking up a hobby, playing a sport, or even exploring new adventures, leisure allows us to embrace our inner child and rediscover the excitement of finding something new.

Banish Boredom and Embrace Variety

Retirement is not a one-way ticket to boredom, but rather an opportunity to explore new horizons. The absence of work-related obligations opens up a whole new world of possibilities, from joining a book club to trying your hand at painting or even traveling to far-flung destinations, leisure gives you the freedom to pursue a myriad of interests. With an ample dose of variety, retirement becomes a thrilling chapter of your life, filled with experiences that can keep you mentally and physically engaged and excited.

Physical and Mental Well-being

They say laughter is the best medicine, and retirement provides the perfect opportunity to embrace it. Engaging in leisure activities promotes physical and mental well-being, helping you to maintain a vibrant and active lifestyle. Whether it's taking a walk in the park, practicing yoga, or participating in a dance class, leisure activities keep your body moving and your mind agile. By staying active, you can fend off the aches and pains that come with age, and maintain a positive outlook on life.

Social Connections and Companionship

Retirement doesn't mean bidding farewell to social interactions; in fact it offers the chance to forge new connections and deepen existing relationships. Leisure activities provide a platform for socializing, whether it's joining a local club, attending community events, or simply organizing get-togethers with friends and neighbors. Sharing common interests and hobbies with others not only brings joy but also fosters a sense of camaraderie and belonging. The friendships made through leisure activities can become an invaluable support system in navigating the ups and downs of retirement.

Escape the Hamster Wheel

One of the greatest perks of retirement is escaping the daily hamster wheel. Remember the endless cycle of meetings, deadlines, and office politics? Retirement is the time to bid adieu to all that stress. Leisure activities offer a welcome escape from the pressures of the past, allowing you to savor the present and find purpose beyond the confines of the workplace. The pursuit of leisure ensures that retirement becomes a journey of self-discovery and personal growth rather than a boringly monotonous existence.

Rediscover Yourself

Retirement provides an ideal opportunity to delve into activities that were previously put on the back burner due to work or family commitments. It's a time to rediscover your passions, hobbies, and talents that may have been neglected over the years. Whether it's picking up a musical instrument, writing a memoir, or learning a new language, retirement gives you the gift of time to nurture your personal aspirations. Leisure activities offer a gateway to self-expression and help you shape the next chapter of your life according to your own desires.

In the grand symphony of life, retirement represents the crescendo, the moment when the melody reaches its peak. It is a chapter of newfound freedom, unburdened by the constraints of work. Embracing leisure activities during retirement is not just about having fun; it's about enhancing your overall well-being, cultivating social connections, and embracing personal growth. So, let us not forget the importance of leisure as we embark on this exciting journey. Let us dance, laugh, and play, for in the world of leisure, we will find the true essence of a fulfilling retirement.

Remember, retirement isn't the end. it's the beginning of a new adventure, and leisure is the magnetic compass that will guide us along the way.

Creating a Balanced Retirement Lifestyle

Retirement is a stage in life that many eagerly anticipate, a time to bid farewell to the daily grind and embrace a new chapter of freedom and relaxation. However, achieving a truly fulfilling retirement requires more than simply lounging by the poolside or binge-watching your favorite TV shows. It demands a deliberate effort to create a balanced retirement lifestyle that encompasses various aspects of personal well-being. In this chapter, we explore the key elements that contribute to a harmonious and meaningful retirement experience.

Physical Health and Well-being

Maintaining good physical health becomes even more important during retirement. Regular exercise plays a vital role in preserving mobility, preventing chronic illnesses, and promoting overall well-being. Engaging in activities such as walking, swimming, or yoga can help keep joints flexible, muscles strong, and cardiovascular health in check. Additionally, adopting a balanced diet filled with nutritious foods provides the necessary fuel to sustain an active and vibrant lifestyle. Prioritizing health screenings and check-ups ensures early detection and effective management of any potential health issues that may arise.

Intellectual Stimulation and Growth

Retirement presents an opportunity to indulge in intellectual pursuits that may have taken a backseat during the hectic grind of our working years. Engaging in activities that stimulate the mind, such as reading books, attending lectures, or taking up new hobbies, can foster continuous learning and personal growth. Exploring new interests or acquiring new skills not only keeps the mind sharp but also gives us a new sense of fulfilment and accomplishment. By embracing intellectual curiosity, a retiree can maintain good mental acuity and contribute to their communities through sharing knowledge and experiences.

Emotional Well-being and Relationships

Looking after emotional well-being is a critical part of creating a balanced retirement lifestyle. Transitioning from a structured and sometimes boring work environment to a more flexible retirement routine can bring about a varied range of emotions. It is important to cultivate positive relationships with loved ones, friends, and peers to garner a sense of belonging and emotional support. Engaging in social activities, joining clubs or community organizations, and volunteering can all contribute to a rich social network that provides companionship, intellectual stimulation, and emotional strength. Additionally, setting aside time for self-reflection, practicing mindfulness, and seeking professional support when needed can contribute to ongoing emotional well-being during retirement.

Financial Planning and Security

A vital component for achieving balance in retirement is establishing financial stability. Careful financial planning ensures that a retiree can sustain their desired lifestyle without undue stress or worry. Creating a comprehensive budget that accounts for living expenses, leisure activities, healthcare costs, and unexpected contingencies helps a retiree manage their finances effectively. Additionally, considering investments, retirement accounts, and potential income streams can provide a steady income during their retirement years. Seeking professional advice from financial planners or retirement experts can offer valuable guidance in making informed decisions and safeguarding financial well-being.

Purpose and Meaningful Engagement

Retirement should not be mistaken for an endless vacation devoid of any purpose. Discovering and pursuing meaningful activities can give a retiree a sense of purpose, fulfilment, and continued useful contribution to society. Engaging in volunteer work, mentoring, or taking up hobbies that align with personal passions can provide a renewed sense of purpose and make a positive impact in the community. Embracing new challenges and setting achievable goals helps to maintain motivation, drive, and a sense of accomplishment.

Creating a balanced retirement lifestyle requires a holistic approach that encompasses physical health, intellectual stimulation, emotional well-being, financial planning, and purposeful engagement. By prioritizing these key aspects, a retiree can embark on a truly fulfilling life at the same time, enjoying a journey that embraces the freedom of retirement while at the same time, building happiness and personal growth.

CHAPTER

13

Cultivating Lifelong Learning

Retirement marks a very significant milestone in life, a period when one bids farewell to the daily grind of work and discovers a newfound freedom. However, it is crucial to recognize that retirement should not equate to idleness. On the contrary, it presents an ideal opportunity to explore and embrace learning in various forms. As we enter this new phase, let us delve into the significance of taking up new learning opportunities and discovering how this can improve and enrich our lives.

Lifelong Learning

Retirement offers the luxury of time that was often extremely limited during our working years. Engaging in new learning activities not only keeps our minds active but also helps us maintain mental agility and sharpness. Lifelong learning has been linked to good cognitive health and overall well-being. By pursuing new knowledge and skills, we can continue to grow and adapt to the ever-changing world around us.

Pursuing Personal Interests

Throughout our working career, we may have had little time to pursue our personal passions or delve deeper into subjects that really interest us. Retirement provides the perfect opportunity to finally explore those interests. Whether it's studying history, learning a foreign language, or diving into literature, we can indulge in the joy of learning without the constraints of a demanding work schedule.

Professional Development

Retirement doesn't necessarily mean the end of our professional development. Many retirees choose to engage in part-time work, consulting, or even starting up their own business venture. In these cases, acquiring new skills and knowledge becomes vital to remaining competitive and staying relevant in the ever-changing fast-moving world we live in. Continuing education courses, workshops, and seminars offer very valuable opportunities to improve our existing expertise or allow us to venture into new fields.

Volunteerism and Community Engagement

Retirement is an ideal time for us to give back to society and make a positive impact on the community we live in. Engaging in volunteer work not only benefits others but also provides a retiree with opportunities to learn and grow. From mentoring programs to working with non-profit organizations, these experiences can open up new challenges and perspectives, fostering personal growth and a deeper understanding of the world around us.

Cultural Enrichment

Travel and cultural exploration are often seen to be synonymous with retirement. By immersing ourselves in different cultures, we can open our minds to diverse perspectives and broaden our horizons. Exploring historical landmarks, visiting museums, attending concerts or theater performances, and engaging in local traditions will allow a retiree to deepen their understanding of the world's rich tapestry of art, history, and heritage.

Technology Adoption

In today's digital age, technology plays a significant role in our daily lives. Retirement provides an excellent opportunity to bridge the digital divide and become more tech-savvy. Learning to navigate social media platforms, effectively use smartphones and tablets, or embrace online learning platforms expands communication channels, facilitates better connections with loved ones, and opens up a wealth of information at our fingertips.

To summarize, retirement is not a time to retreat from the world, but rather a chance to reignite our passion for learning and personal growth. Embracing learning opportunities in retirement not only keeps our minds sharp but also enhances our overall well-being. From exploring personal interests to professional development, volunteering, cultural enrichment, and technological advancements, the possibilities are endless. So, let us embark on this journey of lifelong learning, expanding our knowledge and embracing new experiences, as we taste the many rewards that retirement has to offer.

The Benefits of Continuous Education

Education is the foundation upon which societies thrive and individuals prosper. Traditionally, education has been associated with formal schooling, but in the ever-evolving world we live in, the concept of education has expanded beyond the confines of classrooms and diplomas. Continuous education, also known as lifelong learning, has emerged as a powerful tool for personal and professional growth. In what follows, we will explore the profound benefits of continuous education and why it is an essential pursuit for individuals in today's dynamic world.

Adapting to a Changing World

The pace of change in our modern world is nothing short of breathtaking. Technological advancements, economic shifts, and societal transformations are reshaping industries and job markets. Continuous education equips individuals with the necessary skills and knowledge to adapt and thrive in this rapidly evolving landscape. By embracing lifelong learning, individuals can stay ahead of the curve, remain competitive, and navigate the challenges of an ever-changing world.

Professional Growth and Advancement

In today's competitive environment, a static skill set is no longer sufficient. Continuous education provides professionals and retirees with the means to expand their knowledge base, acquire new skills, and enhance their expertise. By keeping up with industry trends and advancements, an individual can position themself as a valuable asset to their employer, or in retirement, as a highly sought-after expert in their respective field. Continuous education not only opens doors to new in-work opportunities but also paves the way for advancement in possible earning potential in retirement.

Personal Development and Self-Enrichment

Education is not limited to the acquisition of job-related skills alone. Continuous education offers individuals the opportunity to explore diverse subjects, broaden their horizons, and cultivate a deeper understanding of the world around them. Whether it's learning a new language, studying philosophy, or delving into the arts, continuous education enriches one's personal life and fosters intellectual growth. It stimulates critical thinking, enhances problem-solving abilities, and encourages a lifelong love for learning which will be of huge benefit in retirement.

Improved Cognitive Abilities

Engaging in continuous education has been shown to have a positive impact on cognitive abilities and overall mental well-being. Research indicates that learning new skills and engaging in intellectually stimulating activities can improve memory, enhance concentration, and sharpen cognitive function. Just like exercise keeps the body fit, continuous education exercises the mind, keeping the brain agile and alert. It can help stave off cognitive decline and age-related mental disorders, promoting healthy aging with an improved quality of life.

Social Groups and Networking Opportunities

Continuous education provides opportunities for individuals to connect with like-minded individuals, fostering the development of social networks and professional relationships. Whether through in-person classes, workshops, or online communities, lifelong learners can comfortably engage with people from many diverse backgrounds, sharing experiences, ideas, and insights. These interactions not only broaden perspectives but also create networking opportunities that can lead to collaborations, mentorship, and even retirement advancements.

Personal Fulfilment and a Sense of Purpose

There is an inherent satisfaction and fulfilment that comes from the pursuit of knowledge. Continuous education allows individuals to explore their passions, discover new interests, and find a sense of purpose beyond the constraints of their daily routines. It ignites intellectual curiosity, instills a thirst for discovery, and keeps the flame of lifelong learning burning brightly. The joy of personal growth and the pursuit of knowledge bring a deep sense of fulfilment and a richer, more meaningful life experience.

Continuous education is a transformative journey that offers countless benefits for individuals looking for personal growth, professional development, and intellectual enrichment. In a world that demands adaptability and lifelong learning, keeping up with continuous education becomes not just an option but a necessity. By expanding our knowledge, acquiring new skills, and staying intellectually engaged, we unlock a world of possibilities, realizing our true potential and making significant contributions to our personal and professional spheres. Let's embrace the transformative power of continuous education and set out on a journey of lifelong learning, one that enriches our lives and enables us to create a better future.

CHAPTER

14

Dealing with Procrastination Relapses

Relapse is a recurring concern for individuals, whether it be in recovery from an addiction, or simply an unconscious decision to put off what we know we had planned to do, but conveniently find an excuse not to fulfil that intended action. It refers to the resumption of habitual behavior after a period of avoiding procrastination. Relapse can be disheartening and frustrating, but it's important to remember that it is a part of the recovery process for many people. One way to navigate this challenge is to understand the concept of relapse triggers, which are factors that can potentially lead someone back into lethargic or lazy behavior. By recognizing and managing these triggers, individuals can enhance their chances of maintaining long-term activity.

Relapse triggers can be classified into three main categories: internal, external, and environmental. Internal triggers are emotional or psychological factors that arise from within an individual. These triggers can include stress, anxiety, depression, low self-esteem, or unresolved trauma. When faced with these intense emotions, individuals may turn to their lethargy as a coping mechanism, seeking temporary relief or escape from the activity they know they should be pursuing.

External triggers, on the other hand, are external factors that can tempt or influence someone to relapse. These can include being in the presence of someone who takes our attention away from where it should be. Social settings that involve parties or bars, can also act as external triggers. Additionally, certain situations or events such as a too good to miss tv show, or a dog telling us it needs a walk – the list can be as long as you like in order to avoid doing what is necessary.

Environmental triggers refer to the broader context in which an individual lives or works. These triggers include factors such as a lack of social support, unstable relationships, financial stress, or a high-pressure work or home environment. These external stressors can significantly impact an individual's ability to cope with challenges, making them more likely to relapse into procrastinating.

Recognizing one's own personal relapse triggers is crucial for maintaining recovery from procrastination. Self-awareness and honesty are essential in identifying the specific triggers that may lead to relapse. Reflecting on past experiences and noting patterns of behavior can provide valuable insights into the triggers that have been prevalent in the past.

Once triggers have been identified, it's important to develop effective strategies to manage them. Here are some strategies that can help individuals prevent relapse:

Build a strong support network: Surrounding yourself with supportive and understanding individuals can provide a valuable safety net during challenging times. Joining socially supportive groups or seeking advice can offer an opportunity to share experiences, gain encouragement, and learn from others who have successfully navigated similar challenges.

Develop healthy coping mechanisms: Finding alternative ways to manage stress and emotional turmoil is crucial. Engaging in activities such as exercise, meditation, or creative pursuits can provide a healthy outlet for emotions and help redirect focus away from procrastinating.

Practice self-care

Prioritizing self-care is essential for maintaining overall well-being. This includes getting adequate sleep, eating a balanced diet, and engaging in activities that promote relaxation and rejuvenation.

Avoid high-risk situations

If certain situations or events have sometimes acted as triggers in the past, it may be sensible to try to avoid them, especially in the early stages of recovering from a habit of procrastinating. This can minimize exposure to potential relapse triggers and allow for the development of better habits and coping mechanisms.

Create a relapse prevention plan

Working with a therapist or counselor to develop a relapse prevention plan can be quite expensive but highly beneficial. This plan should outline strategies to address each identified trigger, as well as steps to take in case of a relapse. It serves as a roadmap to navigate the challenges of recovery and provides a clear course of action in times of need.

Practice mindfulness

Developing mindfulness skills can help individuals become more aware of their thoughts, emotions, and physical sensations. By staying present in the moment, individuals can better recognize triggers as they arise and consciously choose sensible solutions instead of succumbing to just wanting to sit down and do nothing.

Understanding relapse triggers is a vital aspect of the recovery journey. It allows individuals to anticipate and prepare for potential challenges, empowering them to make informed choices and develop effective coping strategies. By actively managing triggers and seeking support when needed, individuals can enhance their chances of maintaining long-term activity and leading fulfilling lives free from the grip of procrastination. Remember, recovery is a process, and relapse does not signify failure. It is an opportunity to learn, grow, and continue on the path towards a happier and more fulfilling future.

Developing Resilience and Bouncing Back

Here's a gentle guide to overcoming some of life's little challenges.

Life is a journey fraught with unexpected twists, turns, and obstacles that can leave us feeling overwhelmed and defeated. However, within each of us lies the wonderfully incredible power of resilience, the ability to adapt, and the strength to bounce back from adversity. Now we can explore the importance of developing that resilience and provide practical methods or strategies to help you navigate some of those challenges with grit, determination and perseverance.

Embrace Change and Uncertainty

Change is an inherent part of life, and learning to embrace it is crucial for building resilience. Accept that uncertainty is a natural and unavoidable aspect of our existence. By acknowledging that change is constant, we can develop a mindset that is open, adaptable, and prepared for whatever comes our way. Rather than resisting change, let us welcome it as an opportunity for growth and self-discovery.

Cultivate a Supportive Network

During difficult times, the support of others can make all the difference. Surround yourself with a network of friends, family, and mentors who offer encouragement, guidance, and an attentive listening ear. These individuals can provide valuable insights, different perspectives, and emotional support, helping you regain your balance and find the strength to persevere

Practice Self-Care and Well-being

Resilience is not solely about mental fortitude; it also encompasses physical and emotional well-being. Make self-care a priority in your life. Engage in activities that nurture your body and mind, such as exercise, healthy eating, sufficient sleep, and engaging in hobbies or activities that bring you pleasure and joy. Taking care of yourself equips you with the energy and resilience needed to face life's challenges head-on.

Develop Problem-Solving Skills

Resilient individuals possess effective problem-solving skills, enabling them to approach challenges with a proactive mindset. Break down complex problems into smaller, manageable tasks, and develop strategies to tackle them systematically. Look for creative solutions, seek advice from trusted sources, and be willing to adjust your approach if necessary. By developing your problem-solving abilities, you'll build confidence in your ability to overcome obstacles and avoid procrastination.

Practice Optimism and Positive Thinking

Maintaining a positive outlook can significantly impact your resilience. Adopting an optimistic mindset doesn't mean ignoring the difficulties you face; rather, it involves reframing challenges as opportunities for growth and learning. Focus on the lessons you can learn from each experience and the possibilities that lie ahead. By cultivating positive thinking, you'll develop resilience that will sustain you even during the "Oh I'll do it later" moments.

Learn from Failure and Setbacks

Failure is an inevitable part of life, but it doesn't define us. Resilient individuals view failure as an opportunity for growth, learning, and self-improvement. When faced with setbacks, reflect on what went wrong, identify lessons learned, and adjust your approach accordingly. By reframing failures as stepping stones toward success, you'll develop a resilience that enables you to bounce back stronger than ever before.

Cultivate Emotional Intelligence

Emotional intelligence involves recognizing, understanding, and managing your own emotions and empathizing with the emotions of others. Developing emotional intelligence enhances your resilience by enabling you to navigate difficult emotions, maintain healthy relationships, and communicate effectively. By cultivating self-awareness and empathy, you'll build stronger connections and develop a greater capacity for dealing with whatever comes along.

Seek Meaning and Purpose

Discovering meaning and purpose in your life provides a powerful anchor during challenging times. Engage in activities that align with your values, passions, and beliefs. Explore your strengths and talents, and find ways to contribute to something greater than yourself. Having a sense of purpose fosters resilience, as it reminds you of the significance of your journey and the positive impact you can make on the world.

To summarize, developing resilience is a lifelong project, requiring patience, perseverance, and self-discipline. By embracing change, building a supportive network around you, practicing self-care, and honing some problem-solving skills, you can enhance your resilience and more easily bounce back from life's challenges. Remember, resilience is not about avoiding or suppressing difficulties; it's about building the inner strength and adaptability necessary to thrive in the face of adversity. With resilience as your friend and ally, you can navigate life's unpredictable terrain with confidence and determination.

CHAPTER

15

Healthy Habits for Productivity

Retirement marks a significant transition in one's life, offering an opportunity to enjoy newfound freedom and pursue personal interests. However, maintaining a healthy lifestyle remains crucial at all times during this phase of one's life. In fact, adopting good dietary and exercise habits can greatly contribute to overall well-being and productivity during retirement.

We will explore the importance of diet and exercise in supporting a productive retirement and provide practical tips for incorporating these habits into your daily routine.

Nourishing the Body, Fuelling the Mind

A balanced diet forms the foundation of a healthy lifestyle, regardless of age. During retirement, it becomes even more critical to provide the body with the nutrients it needs to function optimally. Incorporating a variety of fresh fruits, vegetables, whole grains, lean proteins, and healthy fats into your meals will ensure a well-rounded and nourishing diet.

Adequate nutrition offers numerous benefits for mental function and cognitive health. Research suggests that certain nutrients, such as omega-3 fatty acids, antioxidants, and B vitamins, play a crucial role in maintaining brain health and memory. By prioritizing a nutrient-rich diet, you can support optimal cognitive function, enhance focus, and improve overall productivity during your retirement years.

The Powerful Benefit of Exercise

Regular physical activity is not only beneficial for maintaining physical fitness but also contributes significantly to mental well-being. Engaging in regular exercise during retirement can boost energy levels, improve mood, reduce stress and anxiety, and enhance cognitive function.

Aerobic exercises, such as brisk walking, swimming, or cycling, help improve cardiovascular health, increase endurance, and promote overall fitness. Strength training exercises, like lifting weights or using resistance bands, are essential for maintaining muscle strength and preventing age-related muscle loss. Engaging in flexibility exercises, such as yoga or stretching, can improve balance, posture, and joint mobility.

By incorporating a combination of aerobic, strength, and flexibility exercises into your routine, you can increase your physical capabilities, feel more energized, and maintain an active and productive lifestyle during retirement.

Establishing Healthy Habits

In order to reap the benefits of a healthy diet and regular exercise, it is essential to establish sustainable habits. Here are a few practical tips to help you incorporate these habits into your retirement routine:

Meal Planning

Plan your meals in advance to ensure a well-balanced and nutritious diet. Include a variety of food groups, focus on portion control, and limit the consumption of processed foods and sugary drinks.

Regular Exercise Schedule

Set aside dedicated time for physical activity each day. Aim for at least 150 minutes of moderate-intensity aerobic activity per week, along with strength training exercises two or more days a week.

Stay Hydrated:

Drinking an adequate amount of water is crucial for maintaining overall health and well-being. Keep a water bottle nearby and sip throughout the day to stay hydrated.

Seek Social Support

Engaging in activities with others can enhance motivation and provide social support. Consider joining exercise classes or groups, or participating in local community events to stay active and connected.

Consult a Professional

If you have specific dietary or exercise concerns, it is advisable to consult with a healthcare professional or a registered dietitian. They can provide personalized guidance and help tailor a plan that suits your individual needs and goals.

As you embark on the journey of retirement, prioritizing your health through diet and exercise can significantly impact your overall well-being and productivity. A balanced diet rich in essential nutrients, combined with regular physical activity, supports optimal cognitive function, boosts energy levels, and enhances mental and physical well-being.

By incorporating healthy habits into your daily routine, such as meal planning, regular exercise, and seeking social support, you can make the most of your retirement years and maintain a high level of productivity. Embrace the opportunity to care for your body and mind, and enjoy the benefits of a healthy and fulfilling retirement journey.

Enhancing Sleep and Rest

Key to productivity in retirement is a cherished phase of life when we leave the daily grind behind us and embrace the freedom to pursue our passions. It is a time to indulge in relaxation and enjoy the fruits of our labor. However, amidst the excitement and newfound leisure, maintaining healthy sleep and rest habits becomes essential for sustaining productivity and overall well-being in retirement. Let's explore the significance of quality sleep and rest and discuss practical strategies to optimize these aspects of our lives during this golden period.

The Importance of Quality Sleep

Sleep is the cornerstone of our physical and mental health. As we age, the quality of our sleep often undergoes changes, making it imperative to prioritize healthy sleep habits in retirement. A good night's sleep promotes cognitive function, memory consolidation, and emotional well-being.

It revitalizes our bodies, allowing us to wake up feeling refreshed and energized to tackle the day's endeavours, without needing to put them off until tomorrow!

Establishing a Sleep Routine

One of the fundamental pillars of healthy sleep is maintaining a consistent sleep routine. Retirement may grant us the luxury of flexibility, but adhering to a regular sleep schedule can work wonders. Aim to go to bed and wake up at the same time each day, aligning your body's natural circadian rhythm. This consistency helps regulate your sleep-wake cycle and promotes a more restful sleep.

Creating a Sleep-Friendly Environment

Crafting a conducive sleep environment is crucial for optimizing the quality of your rest. Begin by ensuring your bedroom is cool, dark, and quiet. Invest in a comfortable mattress and pillows that support your body's needs. Consider using blackout curtains, earplugs, or white noise machines to minimize disruptions that may interrupt your sleep. Transform your bedroom into a tranquil sanctuary dedicated to rejuvenation and relaxation.

Implementing Technology Smartly

While technology can be a double-edged sword when it comes to sleep, it can also offer valuable resources. Avoid using electronic devices such as smartphones, tablets, or laptops right before bedtime as the blue light emitted can interfere with your sleep-wake cycle. Instead, embrace technology for sleep-enhancing purposes. Utilize apps or devices that offer soothing sounds, guided meditations, or white noise to help you unwind and drift into a peaceful slumber.

Nurturing Healthy Sleep Habits

Certain lifestyle choices can significantly impact your sleep quality. Moderate your consumption of caffeine and alcohol, especially in the evening, as they can disrupt sleep patterns. Engage in regular physical activity during the day, as exercise promotes better sleep. However, try to avoid vigorous workouts too close to bedtime, as they can leave you feeling energized and make it harder to fall asleep.

Instigate Relaxation Techniques

Retirement offers an opportune moment to explore various relaxation techniques that can enhance sleep quality. Practices such as deep breathing exercises, progressive muscle relaxation, or meditation can help calm your mind and prepare it for a restful night. Experiment with different techniques to find what works best for you and incorporate them into your evening routine.

Power of Napping

Retirement affords us the freedom to incorporate napping into our daily routine, and when done wisely, it can boost productivity. Short power naps of around 20 minutes can provide a quick recharge, increase alertness, and enhance cognitive function. However, be cautious not to overindulge in napping or nap too close to bedtime, as this may disrupt your regular sleep patterns.

Seeking Professional Assistance

If you find persistent sleep difficulties or suspect an underlying sleep disorder, do not hesitate to seek professional help. Consulting with a healthcare provider or sleep specialist can help identify and address any potential issues that may be affecting your sleep quality. They can provide tailored guidance and recommend appropriate interventions to optimize your restful slumber.

As you set out on your retirement journey, nurturing healthy sleep and rest habits becomes paramount for maintaining productivity and overall well-being. Prioritize the quality of your sleep by establishing a consistent routine, creating a sleep-friendly environment, and incorporating relaxation techniques into your daily life. Embrace the advantages of technology while being mindful of its potential drawbacks. Remember, a well-rested mind and body are the catalysts for a fulfilling and productive retirement. So, embark on this new chapter with the commitment to enhancing your sleep and rest, and unlock the full potential of your golden years.

CHAPTER

16

Enhancing Creativity and Innovation

As already stated, Retirement marks a significant juncture in life, a period when years of dedicated work culminate into a new phase of existence characterized by leisure and the pursuit of personal passions. Engaging in creative hobbies and new projects during retirement offers a unique avenue for self-expression, cognitive stimulation, and a heightened sense of purpose. Here we will look into the profound benefits of immersing oneself in creative endeavors during this transformative stage, exploring how these activities can enrich the retirement experience and contribute to one's overall well-being.

Releasing Cognitive vitality

Retirement need not signal a departure from intellectual engagement; rather, it is a perfect opportunity to embark on new and novel intellectual pursuits. Creative hobbies and new projects serve as mental gymnastics, keeping our cognitive faculties sharp and fully adaptive. The act of learning a new artistic skill, whether it's painting, sculpting, or playing a musical instrument, stimulates our neural pathways, promoting mental agility and resilience. By challenging the brain to process new information and master new and intricate techniques, a retiree can strengthen their cognitive reserves and continue to evolve intellectually

Cultivating Emotional Wellness

Transitioning from a working environment into retirement can trigger an array of emotions, from excitement to uncertainty. Engaging in creative pursuits can offer us an emotional outlet, a space to process our feelings and channel our energy into something new and meaningful. The act of creating, whether it's painting a landscape in oils or making a unique piece of glazed pottery, can give one a sense of accomplishment, pride, and satisfaction. These emotional rewards can contribute to a greater sense of well-being, counteracting any potential feelings of lethargy or aimlessness often associated with retirement.

Nurturing a Sense of Identity and Purpose

For many, retirement can entail a complete recalibration of personal identity, as the roles and responsibilities associated with a working career now have to take a backseat. Creative hobbies and new projects provide a retiree with a platform to establish a new sense of purpose, distinct from that of their previous professional identity. Whether one becomes a skilled woodworker, a prolific writer, or a dedicated gardener, these pursuits will infuse life with purposeful new activities that can contribute to a broader sense of self belief and lasting confidence

Strengthening Social Connections

Retirement often coincides with a shift in social dynamics, as work colleagues become more distant and new daily routines evolve. Engaging in creative hobbies and new projects can serve as a bridge to forming new social connections. Participating in activities such as art classes, writing groups, or community gardening initiatives to name a few, not only offer opportunities for collaboration but also provides a shared interest that can form the basis of meaningful relationships. The sense of friendship and shared achievement that emerges from such creative endeavors can help a retiree establish a robust social network that will enhance their overall quality of life.

Fostering Lifelong Learning

Retirement should not be mistaken for an endpoint; rather, it is a junction in our life that invites a rejuvenated commitment to learning and improving our personal growth. Creative hobbies and new projects offer a chance to explore new horizons and expand one's skill set. The pursuit of undiscovered ability in any new subject must involve continuous regular learning, experimentation, and refinement. This dedication to learning new things, transcends age, reinforcing the notion that retirement is an ongoing journey of discovery and enrichment.

Leaving a Lasting Legacy

Engaging in creative pursuits during retirement contributes to a tangible and enduring legacy. Artwork, literary creations, and handcrafted items are not only a testament to one's personal creativity, but also serve as a way to share one's life experiences and perspectives with present and future generations. These creations become an integral part of one's being, a bridge between past, present, and future that imparts valuable insights and emotions to those who encounter them.

Retirement is a chapter of life that beckons us to embrace our passions, nourish our intellect, and forge new paths of exploration. Engaging in creative hobbies and new projects during this phase of our life offers a vast array of benefits – from intellectual stimulation and emotional well-being to encouraging new social connections and leaving behind a meaningful legacy. As the panoply of retirement unfolds before us, we should grab hold of the opportunity to fill it with our new found creativity, contributing to a richer and more fulfilling way of life that extends well beyond the confines of a traditional and now past career.

Embracing Creative Hobbies and Projects

Retirement marks a significant junction in our life, a period when years of dedicated work morph into a new phase of living characterized by more leisure time and at last, the ability to follow up on our personal interests and passions. Engaging in creative hobbies and new projects during retirement offers a unique avenue for self-expression, cognitive stimulation, and a heightened sense of purpose. Looking into the profoundly advantageous benefits of immersing oneself in creative endeavors during this transformative stage in our life, we can explor how these activities can enrich the retirement experience and greatly contribute to our overall well-being.

Stimulating Curiosity in Retirement

A Path to Lifelong Enrichment in Retirement, often hailed as the twilight of one's working life, is far from a time of stagnation. Instead, it presents a golden opportunity to embark on a new journey – a journey of self-discovery, intellectual exploration, and enriching experiences. Stimulating curiosity during retirement can be a profoundly rewarding endeavor, improving one's mental agility, emotional well-being, and giving a renewed sense of purpose. Looking at the significance of nurturing curiosity in retirement, we can explore practical ways to do so.

Curiosity: A Lifelong Virtue

Curiosity is not merely a trait confined to the vigor of youth; rather, it is a virtue that transcends age. Cultivating curiosity in retirement serves a multitude of purposes, all of which contribute to a fulfilling and meaningful life. Intellectual curiosity, for instance, keeps the mind engaged and active, enhancing our cognitive abilities and staving off mental decline. The pursuit of knowledge, whether through reading, attending lectures, or engaging in thought-provoking discussions, stimulates the brain and feeds a continuous thirst for learning.

Moreover, curiosity nurtures emotional well-being. Exploring new hobbies, interests, and experiences during retirement can inject a fresh perspective and a renewed sense of excitement into our life. This sense of engagement helps build a positive outlook, mitigating the potential feelings of isolation or lack of purpose that can sometimes blight a retirement.

The Benefits of Curiosity

Stimulating curiosity in retirement yields a plethora of benefits, each contributing to a well-rounded and fulfilling life.

Enhanced Mental Acuity: Engaging in intellectually stimulating activities, such as solving puzzles, learning a new language, or delving into history, challenges the brain and helps maintain cognitive function.

Emotional Resilience: Curiosity-driven exploration encourages adaptability and resilience. It allows retirees to approach change with a more open and adaptable mindset, reducing the stress often associated with life transitions.

Social Connection: Pursuing curiosity often involves interacting with like-minded individuals who share similar interests. Joining clubs, attending workshops, or participating in community events can facilitate new friendships and foster a sense of belonging.

Personal Fulfilment: The pursuit of curiosity often leads to the discovery of hidden passions and talents. Engaging in activities that align with these newfound interests can provide a profound sense of personal fulfilment.

Sense of Purpose: Curiosity fuels a sense of purpose by encouraging retirees to set goals, explore new horizons, and continuously seek personal growth.

Explore New Subjects

Retirement is an ideal time to explore topics you've always been curious about. Enrol in classes or workshops, attend lectures, or look into online courses to deepen your understanding of the subjects that spark your interest.

Read Widely

Reading is a gateway to endless knowledge. Dive into books, articles, and research those that intrigue you, expanding your perspective and opening new areas of interest.

Travel and Discovery

Travel offers an an opportunity to experience new cultures, countries, and traditions. Awake your dormant curiosity to explore different parts of the world and gain a broader understanding of global diversity.

Creative Expression

Engage in creative endeavors such as writing, painting, music, or photography. These outlets encourage self-expression and provide a brilliant platform for exploring new forms of creativity. This is how this book came into being – eventually!

Join Interest Groups

Connect with local clubs, groups, or online communities centered around your interests. Engaging in discussions, sharing insights, and collaborating with others can ignite curiosity-driven conversations.

Mindfulness and Reflection

Practicing mindfulness and self-reflection can help you tap into your inner thoughts and desires. Reflective thinking practices will encourage curiosity about your own motivations, values, and aspirations.

Volunteer and Mentor

Give or share your expertise and experience to the community by volunteering or mentoring others. Such efforts will give you a sense of purpose while allowing you to learn from others while exchanging your knowledge with them.

The Never-Ending Search

Curiosity is a journey that knows no bounds, and retirement provides the blank canvas upon which your journey can be painted with all the vibrant colors your mind can conjure up. The pursuit of knowledge, the exploration of new interests, and the engagement with the world around you will contribute to a life rich in experiences and personal growth. Embrace the opportunity that retirement offers, to satisfy your curiosity and chart a course of continual discovery.

Retirement need not be a period marked by complacency or disengagement. On the contrary, it is a time ripe with the potential for intellectual, emotional, and personal enrichment. By stimulating curiosity and embracing a mindset of exploration, a retiree can embark on a fulfilling path that promises a lifetime of learning, growth, and discovery. So, as you step into the realm of retirement, let curiosity be your faithful guide, leading you toward the untrodden avenues of knowledge and the boundless landscapes of human experience.

CHAPTER

17

Time Management Tools and Apps

Retirement marks a significant transition in one's life, opening doors to newfound freedom and opportunities. As you embark on this chapter in your life, embracing technology can be a key factor in making the most of your time and maintaining an organized and fulfilling lifestyle. Productivity apps have evolved to cater to individuals of all ages, and a retired user is no exception. Now we will explore a range of productivity apps designed to empower anyone to manage their schedules, pursue their hobbies, stay mentally and physically active, and ensure their overall well-being.

Make Your Digital Notebooks

'Evernote.com' https://evernote.com is a versatile note-taking application which can become an indispensable tool for retirees looking to keep track of important information, jot down thoughts, and organize their ideas. Whether it's planning a trip, recording recipes, or preserving cherished memories. This app provides a digital space to declutter the mind and keep things organized. It has a user-friendly interface allowing the user to effortlessly create notebooks, tag entries, and synchronize data across different devices.

Master Your To-Do List

Retirement often brings a myriad of activities and projects. *'Todoist'* https://todoist.com *(there is no l in the name)* is a task management application from 'Monday.com' https://monday.com that helps one prioritize tasks, set deadlines, and ensure that nothing falls through the cracks to be forgotten. With its intuitive design and customizable features, *'Todoist'* aids in managing daily routines, appointments, and even pursuing new hobbies. By visualizing tasks and goals, a retiree can maintain a sense of accomplishment and purpose in their retirement journey.

Nurturing Mental Wellness

Retirement offers an ideal opportunity to focus on mental well-being.

'Headspace', https://headspace.com is a meditation and mindfulness application, which guides the user through exercises to alleviate stress, improve sleep, and enhance focus. As a retiree embraces a slower pace of life, cultivating mindfulness can lead to a more fulfilling and serene retirement experience. *'Headspace'* provides an array of meditation practices tailored to different needs, promoting mental clarity and emotional balance.

Stay Active and Healthy

Physical health remains a cornerstone of a vibrant retirement. *'Fitbit'*, https://www.fitbit.com , a well-known fitness app, enables the user to monitor their activity levels, set fitness goals, and track progress. Through its step-counting, heart rate monitoring, and sleep tracking features, *'Fitbit'* encourages users to maintain an active lifestyle. By staying attuned to their physical well-being, retirees can enjoy their retirement years with vigor and vitality.

Rediscovering the Joy of Reading

'Libby', https://libbyapp.com , an e-book and audiobook application, rekindles the love for reading and learning. With access to a vast digital library, retirees can explore a wide range of literature, from classic novels to non-fiction gems. Audiobooks offer a convenient way to absorb knowledge and stories while engaging in other activities, making *'Libby'* an ideal companion for long walks, leisurely drives, or simply relaxing at home.

Bridging the Distance

In an era of increased digital communication, staying connected with loved ones is essential. *'Zoom'*, https://zoom.us, a video conferencing app, enables users to engage in virtual gatherings, reunions, and conversations with family and friends around the world. It's a valuable tool for maintaining social connections, sharing experiences, and celebrating life's special moments, even from afar.

Embrace Language Learning

Retirement invites a retiree to explore new horizons, and learning a new language can be an extremely fulfilling endeavor. *'Duolingo'*, a language-learning application, https://www.duolingo.com, provides interactive lessons and exercises that cater to various proficiency levels. Whether planning a future trip or simply expanding your cognitive horizons, you can embark on a linguistic journey that stimulates the mind and enhances your cultural awareness.

Retirement is a time of life characterized by newfound freedom and opportunities, and productivity apps offer us a means to make the most of this time. From organizing schedules and tasks to nurturing mental and physical well-being, these apps empower us to lead purposeful and fulfilling lives. As retirees embrace the digital age, integrating these productivity apps into their routine can enhance their overall quality of life and ensure that their retirement years are marked by productivity, enrichment, and joy. By harnessing the capabilities of technology, we can navigate this new phase with confidence and enthusiasm, embracing the endless possibilities that lie ahead.

Navigating Life's Complexity:

The Power of Digital Organizers and Calendars. in the age of information overload and multitasking, helps us with keeping track of our commitments, tasks, and appointments, which has become an increasingly challenging problem. The digital organizers and calendars, are the modern-day tools that have revolutionized the way we manage our lives. In this era of technological advancement, these digital companions offer not just convenience, but a comprehensive solution to the intricate web of responsibilities that are a part of our daily routines.

The Digital Renaissance

Gone are the days of paper planners and wall calendars, where penmanship and manual updates were the norm. The digital renaissance has ushered in a new era, where our lives are meticulously organized and managed with the tap of a keyboard or touch-screen. Digital organizers and calendars have seamlessly integrated themselves into our lives, becoming almost indispensable tools for professionals, students, and anyone, including of course the newly retired seeking to maintain a semblance of order in a perpetually changing world.

Efficiency at Your Fingertips

At the heart of the digital organizer lies its supreme ability to enhance efficiency. These applications offer features that streamline the process of task management, enabling users to create to-do lists, set reminders, and prioritize activities with ease. The seamless synchronization across devices ensures that you are always connected to your schedule, allowing you to seamlessly transition with a smartphone from your desktop to your sofa without missing a beat.

Calendars, whether daily, weekly, or monthly, provide a visual representation of your commitments. The ability to color-code appointments, meetings, and personal events not only adds an aesthetic touch but also offers a quick snapshot of your time allocations. This visual aid helps in optimizing your schedule, enabling you to allocate time to high-priority tasks and strike a balance in your now hopefully busy retirement.

Never Miss a Beat

One of the most significant advantages of digital organizers and calendars is their proactive nature. These tools act as reliable guardians of your time, sending timely reminders, notifications and alerts to make sure that you should never miss a family, social, or medical appointment or deadline again. With the ability to set customizable reminders, you can be assured that important tasks will never be forgotten. Moreover, these digital companions offer the luxury of being able to automatically register recurring events, a feature that eliminates the need to manually input repetitive activities. Whether it's a weekly social meeting or a monthly bill to be paid, the calendar's recurrence function ensures that routine tasks are accounted for, saving you time and mental stress.

Collaboration and Connectivity

In an increasingly interconnected world, collaboration is key. Digital organizers and calendars have risen to the challenge by giving us the ability to seamlessly collaborate with individuals and groups. Shared calendars allow users to coordinate schedules effortlessly, minimizing scheduling conflicts and improving overall productivity. This collaborative aspect can greatly help family life, where family members can synchronize their calendars to stay informed about each other's commitments and social activities.

The Power of Data Insight

Beyond their organizational ability, digital organizers and calendars are able to provide a smorgasbord of available data insights. These tools generate reports and analytics that offer a comprehensive overview of your time allocation, trends, and areas that may require change or improvement. Armed with this information, you can make informed decisions about time management, identify patterns, and optimize your daily routine for peak efficiency.

Mental Liberation

The psychological impact of using digital organizers and calendars is profound. The weight of remembering every task, appointment and birthday, anniversary etc.is lifted, allowing you to focus your mental energy on more creative and strategic pursuits. The reduced stress associated with forgetting important appointments or commitments contributes to a sense of greater control and empowerment, positively impacting your overall well-being.

Cultivating Discipline and Consistency

The act of consistently updating and maintaining a digital organizer or calendar fosters discipline and accountability. The regular engagement with your schedule reinforces the habit of planning, enabling you to allocate time wisely and avoid procrastination. Over time, this discipline becomes ingrained, leading to improved time management skills that extend to all facets of our everyday life.

Embracing the Future

As technology continues to evolve, digital organizers and calendars are almost certain to become even more sophisticated and intuitive. The integration of artificial intelligence and machine learning promises to deliver personalized insights and recommendations, further enhancing the user experience. With the potential to seamlessly integrate with other productivity tools and applications, these digital companions are set to redefine the way we approach organizing our overall time management.

In a world where time is a finite resource and demands are ceaseless, the role of digital organizers and calendars cannot be overstated. These tools have evolved from mere applications to indispensable companions, guiding us through the intricate maze of modern life. With their efficiency, collaborative capabilities, and psychological benefits, digital organizers and calendars give us the power to navigate life's complexities with a certain amount of grace and purpose. As we look to the future, these digital allies will continue to be our partners in the ever-increasing quest for balance, productivity, and fulfilment.

CHAPTER

18

Cultivating a Growth Mindset

Life is a journey filled with twists and turns, surprises and uncertainties. In the intricate complexity of our existence, two constants stand out: change and challenges. Both are inevitable companions on our journey through time, and how we embrace them can shape the very course of our lives. It is through our willingness to confront these forces head-on that we discover the depths of our resilience, strength, and capacity for growth.

Change, the ever-present force of transformation, can be exhilarating, infuriating and often intimidating. It sweeps in like a gust of wind, rearranging the familiar landscape of our lives with a quiet but persistent determination. While change often forces us to step out of our comfort zone, it is also the catalyst for innovation and progress. Embracing change requires a mindset shift – a willingness to let go of the safety of the known and join in the uncertainty of the new.

The journey of embracing change begins with acceptance. It is a realization that the only constant in life is change itself. Seasons change, relationships evolve, and circumstances shift. Rather than resisting this natural rhythm, we must learn to adapt, adopt and flow with it. Just as a tree bends with the wind to avoid breaking, we too must learn to bend without breaking in the face of change.

Challenges, on the other hand, are the crucibles in which our character is tested and refined. They come in various forms – personal, professional, emotional, and physical. Challenges push us beyond our perceived limits, forcing us to dig deep within ourselves for untapped reserves of strength and courage. While they may seem daunting at first, challenges offer unique opportunities for growth and self-discovery.

The key to embracing challenges lies in our perspective. Rather than seeing them as insurmountable obstacles, we can choose to view them as stepping stones towards personal development. Challenges provide a chance to develop problem-solving skills, resilience, and a heightened sense of self-awareness. Just as a sculptor, chips away at a block of marble to reveal a masterpiece, challenges allow us to chisel away at our limitations and reveal the potential within ourselves.

Welcoming change and challenges requires a mindset rooted in positivity and a commitment to personal growth. It entails having the ability to see beyond our immediate discomfort and become aware of the long-term benefits. By viewing challenges as opportunities for learning, we transform adversity into a catalyst for positive change. Every setback becomes a setup for a comeback, and every trial becomes a stepping stone toward a stronger and wiser self.

To embrace change and challenges, we must also cultivate a sense of adaptability. Life rarely follows a linear path, and our ability to pivot and adjust to new circumstances is crucial. This adaptability is not a sign of weakness but rather a testament to our resilience and resourcefulness. Just as a river finds its way around obstacles, we too can navigate the twists and turns of life with grace and determination.

In the face of change and challenges, self-care becomes paramount. Taking care of our physical, mental, and emotional well-being equips us with the strength and clarity needed to navigate tumultuous waters. Engaging in practices such as mindfulness, meditation, and exercise can help us maintain a balanced perspective and foster a sense of inner calm amidst external turbulence.

Ultimately, embracing change and challenges is a lifelong journey – a continuous process of growth and self-discovery. It requires a willingness to step outside our comfort zone, confront our fears, and adapt to the evolving pattern of our life. By viewing change as a natural part of life and challenges as opportunities for growth, we set free our potential to lead fulfilling, purpose-driven lives.

In the everchanging tapestry of life, change and challenges are the threads that weave together our personal and collective experiences. Embracing them allows us to evolve, transform, and transcend our limitations. As we navigate the intricate balance between change and challenges, let us do so with conviction, courage, and an unwavering commitment to becoming the very best version of ourselves.

Developing a Positive Outlook in Retirement

Retirement is a phase of life that marks the culmination of decades of hard work and dedication, which presents a unique opportunity for us to cultivate a positive and fulfilling outlook. While the prospect of stepping away from a structured routine and familiar responsibilities might seem daunting, a deliberate focus on maintaining a positive perspective on life can significantly enhance our retirement experience. In this section we delve into the strategies and insights that can help in developing a constructive and optimistic mindset during this transformative part of our life.

Embrace Change as an Inevitable Constant

The transition into retirement often entails a multitude of changes – from adjusting to a new routine to redefining one's sense of identity. Embracing change as an inevitable part of life can pave the way for a positive outlook. Just as adapting to new roles and responsibilities was a constant in one's working years, embracing the evolving nature of retirement can lead to a sense of renewed purpose. Viewing change as an opportunity for growth rather than a challenge can foster resilience and positivity.

Cultivate Meaningful Social Connections

The importance of social connections in retirement cannot be overstated. Transitioning from a working environment with daily colleague interactions to a more isolated setting can lead to feelings of loneliness. Cultivating and nurturing relationships with friends, family, and even forging new connections within community groups or social clubs can contribute to a sense of belonging and emotional well-being. Engaging in regular social activities can foster a positive sense of camaraderie and provide avenues for meaningful conversations and shared experiences.

Set Realistic Goals and Pursue Passions

Retirement is an ideal time to explore passions and interests that may have taken a backseat during our working years. Setting realistic goals, whether they involve travel, volunteer work, or pursuing a new hobby, can provide a sense of purpose and structure. Engaging in activities that resonate with our personal interests not only enriches our daily life but also contributes to a positive mindset, as the pursuit of passions often leads to a deep and satisfying sense of fulfilment.

Prioritize Physical and Mental Well-being

Maintaining good physical health is closely linked to mental well-being. Regular exercise, a balanced diet, and sufficient sleep can improve mood and energy levels. Engaging in physical activities tailored to individual preferences and capabilities can contribute to a positive outlook by promoting overall vitality and a sense of accomplishment. Additionally, prioritizing mental health through mindfulness practices, meditation, and engaging in intellectually stimulating activities can foster a sense of mental clarity and emotional wellbeing.

Practice Gratitude and Mindfulness

Making a habit of gratitude and mindfulness can significantly influence one's perspective on retirement. Reflecting on the aspects of life that bring joy, expressing gratitude for everyday blessings, and living in the present moment can enhance feelings of contentment. By cultivating an attitude of mindfulness, individuals can savor the richness of their experiences and maintain a positive focus on the present, rather than dwelling on past regrets, or anxieties about the future.

Engage in Lifelong Learning

Retirement does not signify an end to learning, in fact it offers a unique opportunity to engage in lifelong learning endeavors. Exploring new subjects, enrolling in classes, or pursuing online courses can stimulate cognitive functions and maintain mental agility. The process of acquiring new knowledge and skills can create a sense of accomplishment and contribute to a positive self-perceptive mind.

Contribute to the Community

Engaging in volunteer work or community service can play a pivotal role in developing a positive outlook in retirement. Contributing to the well-being of others fosters a sense of purpose and satisfaction. The act of giving back to the community not only strengthens social connections but also reinforces the belief that retirement is a period ripe with opportunities to make a meaningful impact.

Developing a positive outlook in retirement requires a conscious and deliberate approach. By embracing change, cultivating social connections, pursuing passions, prioritizing well-being, practicing gratitude, engaging in lifelong learning, and contributing to the community, individuals can shape their retirement experience into a fulfilling and optimistic journey. While retirement marks a transition from one chapter of life to another, it is a chapter that holds the potential for personal growth, meaningful connections, and the cultivation of a positive and enriching perspective.

CHAPTER

19

Financial Planning and Goal Alignment

Procrastination and retirement planning are often uneasy bedfellows. Many retirees find themselves in a position where the urgency of planning was overshadowed by the comfort of postponing those critical financial decisions. However, it's never too late to take control and align your financial goals with your retirement lifestyle. This chapter aims to guide you through the essentials of financial planning and goal alignment, tailored specifically for those who have put off these important tasks.

Procrastination in retirement planning is not uncommon, but it's never too late to take control. By understanding your financial situation, by setting realistic goals, creating a flexible budget, adopting appropriate investment strategies, and seeking professional help, you can align your finances with your retirement goals. Remember, the key is to start now, no matter how delayed your planning might feel. Taking small, consistent steps can lead to a secure and fulfilling retirement.

Crafting a Solid Foundation

Retirement is that stage of life where the days of grinding work come to a halt and the prospect of endless leisurely pursuits beckons. But without a well-crafted retirement plan, this golden phase could lose its allure. To ensure a financially secure retirement, a structured and thoughtful approach is essential. In this guide, we'll look at the key steps to create a robust retirement plan that safeguards your financial future.

Set Clear Goals

Like any journey, the path to a secure retirement starts with a clear destination. Determine your retirement goals – do you want to travel the world, maintain your current lifestyle, or dedicate more time to hobbies? These aspirations will serve as your compass, guiding your financial decisions along the way.

Calculate Your Retirement Needs

Calculating the amount of money you'll need in retirement is a critical step. Consider your anticipated living expenses, including housing, healthcare, transportation, and discretionary spending. Take inflation into account to ensure that your retirement funds retain their purchasing power over time.

Start Early

Time is a valuable asset when it comes to retirement planning. The earlier you start saving, the more you can leverage the power of compound interest. Even small contributions made consistently over a long period can lead to substantial growth. Procrastination could significantly limit your options down the road.

Maximize Retirement Accounts

Employer-sponsored retirement pension accounts, provide tax advantages and potential employer matches. Contribute enough to take full advantage of any employer contribution

– it's essentially free money. Additionally, Individual Retirement Accounts offer tax-advantaged growth and various investment options.

Diversify Investments

A diversified investment portfolio helps manage risk and enhances the potential for consistent growth. Allocate your investments across various asset classes, such as stocks, bonds, and real estate. Regularly rebalance your portfolio to maintain your desired asset allocation.

Understand Social Security

Social Security benefits play a significant role in many retirees' income streams. Understand how the benefit calculations work and the optimal time to start receiving benefits. Delaying benefits can lead to higher monthly payouts, but the right choice depends on your individual circumstances.

Manage Debt

Carrying significant amounts of debt into retirement can strain your finances and personal relationships. Prioritize paying off high-interest debts, such as credit card balances and personal loans. Reducing debt not only frees up cash flow but also reduces the financial burden on your retirement funds.

Healthcare Planning

Healthcare expenses tend to rise as you age. Medicare, the federal health insurance program for retirees, becomes available at age 65 but this may increase in time. Research Medicare options and consider supplemental insurance plans to cover potential gaps in cover.

Long-Term Care Considerations

Long-term care costs, including assisted living or nursing home care, can be substantial. While not everyone will require long-term care, it's prudent to explore insurance options or alternative funding sources to ensure you're prepared for any eventuality. Regularly Review your needs and adjust things as necessary.

Here in more detail, are the actions you need to be aware of:

Understanding Your Financial Situation

The first step in any financial planning process is understanding where you stand. For procrastinators, this might seem daunting, but breaking it down into manageable steps can make it more approachable.

Assess Your Assets and Liabilities

Assets: List all your savings accounts, investment portfolios, properties, and other valuables.

Liabilities: Note down any debts, including mortgages, personal loans, and credit card balances.

By understanding your net worth (assets minus liabilities), you can get a clear picture of your financial standing.

Analyze Your Income Sources

Social Security: Determine your benefits and when the best time to start claiming them is.

Pensions and Annuities: Review any employer-provided pensions or purchased annuities.

Investments: Evaluate income from dividends, interest, and other investment returns.

Track Your Expenses

Regularly document your monthly and yearly expenses to understand your spending patterns. This includes essentials like housing, healthcare, groceries, and discretionary spending like travel and entertainment.

Set Realistic Goals

Setting goals is critical to aligning your financial plan with your desired lifestyle. Goals give you direction and purpose, making the planning process more tangible and less overwhelming.

Short-Term Goals

Examples include setting up an emergency fund, paying off high-interest debt, or making small home improvements. These goals can be achieved within a year or two and provide immediate financial relief and satisfaction.

Medium-Term Goals

These might include travel plans, purchasing a new car, or funding a grandchild's education. These goals typically span 3-5 years and require a moderate level of planning and saving.

Long-Term Goals

Long-term goals focus on sustaining your lifestyle throughout your retirement. This includes making sure you have sufficient funds for healthcare, long-term care, and maintaining your desired standard of living.

Create a Flexible Budget

A flexible budget adapts to changes in income and expenses, which is particularly important for a retiree. It helps you manage your money effectively and allows for adjustments as needed.

Essential Expenses

Prioritize necessary expenses like housing, utilities, groceries, and healthcare. These should be covered by your guaranteed income sources such as Social Security benefits or pensions.

Discretionary Spending

Allocate funds for discretionary spending, including hobbies, travel, and dining out. This category can be adjusted more easily if financial circumstances change.

Emergency Fund

Ensure you have an emergency fund to cover unexpected expenses. This fund should ideally cover 3-6 months of living expenses and be easily accessible.

Investment Strategies

Even in retirement, investment strategies are crucial for growing or maintaining your wealth. Procrastinators might be wary of complex investment plans, but simplicity can be highly effective.

Risk Assessment

Evaluate your risk tolerance. Generally, as you age, a more conservative investment approach is advisable, but some exposure to growth assets can help combat inflation.

Diversification

Diversify your investments to reduce risk. This includes a mix of stocks, bonds, and other asset classes. The old adage 'never keep all your eggs in one basket' is very sound advice.

Regular Review

Periodically review your investment portfolio to ensure it aligns with your goals and adjust it as necessary. Working with a financial advisor can be beneficial if you're uncertain about making these adjustments yourself, but remember such help may cost you.

Seek Professional Help

If the thought of financial planning feels overwhelming, seeking professional help can be a wise decision. Financial advisors can provide personalized advice and help you develop a comprehensive retirement plan, but as above, remember it will likely not be free.

Find a Fiduciary Advisor

Look for advisors who are fiduciaries, meaning they are legally obligated to act in your best interest.

Discuss Your Goals and Concerns

Be open about your financial situation, goals, and any procrastinatory habits. Transparency helps advisors create a plan tailored to your needs and abilities.

Check-In Regularly

Schedule regular meetings with your advisor to review your plan and make any necessary adjustments.

A retirement plan isn't a static document – it should evolve as your circumstances change. Review your plan periodically to ensure it remains aligned with your goals. Life events like marriage, the birth of children, or changes in income should prompt a reassessment of your plan's effectiveness.

Estate Planning

Establishing an estate plan is essential to ensure your assets are distributed according to your wishes. Create a will, identify beneficiaries for your retirement accounts, and consider setting up trusts if necessary. Estate planning helps minimize taxes and simplifies the transfer of assets to your heirs.

Do Seek Professional Guidance

Navigating the complexities of retirement planning can be daunting. Consulting with a certified financial planner or retirement advisor can provide invaluable insights and they'll tailor a plan that aligns with your unique circumstances and objectives.

In conclusion, creating a financially secure retirement plan demands careful consideration, disciplined saving, and a commitment to ongoing adjustments. It's a journey that requires foresight, knowledge, and diligence.

By following these steps and making informed decisions, you can pave the way to a retirement that's financially comfortable and emotionally fulfilling. Remember, the choices you make today will determine the quality of life you enjoy during your well-earned retirement years.

CHAPTER

20

Conclusion

Retirement, once a milestone often associated with the notion of winding down and taking a step back from life's demands, has undergone a significant transformation over recent years. The traditional image of a retired person idly passing their days doing little, or nothing, has given way to a new perspective—one that encourages individuals to embark on a proactive retirement lifestyle, enriched with endless opportunities for personal growth, meaningful engagement, and continued contribution to society.

As the last chapter of one's professional journey unfolds, the question of how to make the most of this newfound freedom becomes increasingly relevant. Embracing a proactive retirement lifestyle signifies more than a departure from the conventional; it heralds in a significant shift towards an intentional and purpose-driven existence, ensuring that one's golden retirement years are characterized by vitality, fulfilment, and an enduring sense of purpose.

The Power of Purposeful Pursuits

Retirement should not be viewed as a retreat from the world, but rather an invitation to explore new horizons and unearth passions that may have taken a backseat during the busy years of a working career. Engaging in purposeful pursuits after retiring can provide a profound sense of fulfilment and satisfaction. Whether it's embarking on a long dreamed of creative endeavor, getting involved in charitable efforts, or pursuing further education, these activities give purpose and invigoration in life. Moreover, adopting a proactive approach to retirement can enhance mental and emotional well-being. The engagement associated with purposeful pursuits improves cognitive vitality and helps stave off the potential challenges caused by cognitive decline. It's a positive stand against complacency, enabling a retiree to maintain a sharp mind and an active healthy lifestyle.

Continued Learning

Retirement is a time in life where the search for knowledge and personal growth can flourish. Lifelong learning isn't restricted to the boundaries of a classroom; it covers a broad array of opportunities. From attending workshops or seminars to following an online course or engaging in literary discussions, a retiree can continuously expand their horizons.

Such dedication to learning not only enriches our personal experiences but also establishes a way for connecting with like-minded individuals. It opens the door to previously unknown social circles, creating new relationships based on shared interests and the pursuit of knowledge. In a proactive retirement, the thirst for knowledge remains, pushing individuals toward a life of constant discovery.

Physical and Mental Well-Being

A proactive lifestyle in retirement extends beyond mental pursuits; it includes the making of improved physical well-being. Engaging in regular exercise, maintaining a balanced diet, and prioritizing one's healthcare contribute to a vibrant retirement life. Staying physically active maintains and enhances mobility, strengthens the immune system, and contributes to our overall longevity.

Additionally, looking after mental health is paramount. Retirement can bring about sysmic shifts in identity and a sense of purpose, potentially leading to feelings of isolation or inadequacy. Engaging in mindfulness practices, seeking appropriate therapy, or participating in support groups can help overcome these challenges, building resilience and emotional well-being.

Giving Back

Retirees have a wealth of experience, knowledge, and skills that can benefit society long after they leave the work place. Keeping to a proactive retirement lifestyle can often involve seeking ways to give back to the community. Volunteering for charitable organizations, mentoring younger generations, or taking part in advocacy work, allows a retiree to channel their knowledge and expertise toward meaningful activities.

Contributing to the well-being of others not only gives a sense of purpose but also reinforces the idea that retirement represents a transition, not an end. By sharing their insights and resources, retirees play an active role in shaping the future and leaving a lasting legacy.

Cultivating Social Connections

Maintaining robust social connections is a vital part of a proactive lifestyle in retirement. Human beings are inherently social creatures, and interactions with others have a profound impact on general well-being. Cultivating new friendships, participating in group activities, and engaging in social clubs can help combat feelings of isolation and loneliness that sometimes accompany retirement.

Furthermore, these connections can provide opportunities for intellectual stimulation, emotional support, and the exchange of diverse ideas. Active engagement in social circles fosters a sense of belonging and contributes to a more holistic and fulfilling retirement.

Forging the Next Chapter of your life

Embracing a proactive retirement lifestyle is a deliberate choice; one that shows a commitment to personal growth, continued learning, and meaningful contribution to society. The traditional notion of retirement as a period of rest has evolved into a dynamic phase of life characterized by purposeful pursuits and activity.

As individuals navigate the transition from the work place to retirement, the prospect of a proactive lifestyle calls as an opportunity to reimagine their life. By prioritizing physical and mental well-being, encouraging social connections, and giving back to the community, a retiree can create a life that defies convention and embraces the full array of their potential.

Celebrating the Fulfilment of Accomplishments

Retirement is a chapter in life that marks the culmination of years of hard work, dedication, and perseverance in the work place. It is a time of transition that allows individuals to reflect on their accomplishments and find a satisfying sense of fulfilment. As the curtains draw on the professional stage, retirement unveils a new scene, rich with opportunities for personal growth, exploration, and the deep satisfaction that comes from a life well-lived. In this, we relish the joy of accomplishment and fulfilment leading up to and during retirement, discovering the essence of this remarkable phase of life.

The path leading up to retirement is often paved with milestones and achievements that define one's career and personal growth. From the first hesitant steps into the professional world to the ultimate mastery of skills that shaped our industries, each achievement contributes to a sense of purpose and fulfilment. Whether it's climbing the corporate ladder, making groundbreaking scientific discoveries, or training the next generation as an educator, these accomplishments create a broad tapestry of experiences that meld into the very fabric of a successfully fulfilling life.

The sheer joy of accomplishment is deeply ingrained in the knowledge that one's efforts have made a lasting impact to be seen by those around us. It is a feeling of pride that comes from knowing that you have contributed to a larger purpose, leaving an indelible mark on the world. For many, the journey to retirement is a period of reflection, a time to appreciate the significance of their achievements and the role they have played in shaping their respective area of competence.

Transitioning into Fulfilment

Retirement is not an endpoint, but rather a gateway to a new phase of existence. As individuals step away from their professional roles, they are presented with an opportunity to explore avenues that bring them personal fulfilment. This may involve pursuing long-held passions, engaging in creative endeavors, or embarking on new adventures that were once put on hold due to professional commitments.

During retirement, the joy of fulfilment is found in the pursuit of one's interests without the constraints of working time and business responsibilities. Whether it's dedicating hours to cultivating a garden, volunteering for a cause close to our heart, or traveling to foreign destinations, this phase of life allows retirees to delve into activities that nurture the soul and ignite a new sense of purpose. It is a time to prioritize personal wellbeing and engage in experiences that bring a sense of contentment and satisfaction.

Rediscovering Relationships

Retirement also offers the space and time to rekindle and strengthen relationships that may have been somewhat neglected during the busy years of professional life. It is a period to connect with family members, old friends, and loved ones, sharing experiences and creating lasting memories. The joy of accomplishment and fulfilment extends to the bonds that are formed and promoted during this period, as individuals have the new found leisure time to invest in meaningful interactions.

Retirement provides one an opportunity to become a beacon of support and wisdom for the younger generations, passing down valuable life lessons and experiences. Whether through storytelling, mentoring, or simply spending quality time, retirees can impart a sense of continuity and guidance that enriches the lives of those around them. In doing so, they find fulfilment in the role of a knowledgeable and cherished mentor, perpetuating a legacy that extends way beyond their professional achievements.

Amid following newfound passions and the rekindling of relationships, retirement offers a space for contemplation and self-discovery. It is a time to reflect on the journey that led to this point, acknowledging the challenges we overcame, the lessons learned, and the personal growth experienced along the way. The joy of accomplishment and fulfilment is magnified as a retiree takes stock of their lives, recognizing the richness of their experiences and the wisdom gained from navigating the many complexities of our life.

Through reflection, retirees may find a renewed sense of purpose that transcends the confines of a professional environment. Retirement is a time to explore the deeper dimensions of life, seeking meaning in the connections between personal values, aspirations, and contributions to society. As the canvas of life unfolds, you can find fulfilment in aligning your actions with your innermost convictions, creating a harmony that resonates with a sense of satisfactory completeness.

The journey to retirement is a testament to the power of dedication, perseverance, and a relentless pursuit of excellence. As individuals transition into this phase of their life, they find themselves at the crossroads of accomplishment and fulfilment, ready to embark on a new journey of self-discovery and exploration. The joy derived from a life of achievements is beautifully complemented by the deep satisfaction that comes from following one's passions, strengthening new and old relationships, and reflecting on the many and varied experiences that shape one's legacy.

Now a final word for you, the reader of my book. Retirement is a blank canvas just waiting to be painted with the colors of your personal fulfilment, purpose, and contentment. It is a time to savor the fruits of your previous labor and embrace the boundless opportunities that lie ahead. With each day of retirement, you will have the privilege of writing a new chapter of your life that celebrates the joy of your successfully completed accomplishments, leaving an indelible mark on your own heart and the hearts of others who know you.

Go forward, do things, don't look back, meet people, and above all, keep doing stuff that keeps your body and your brain active.

Remember that the harder you try, the more successful you will become and better things will come your way. Just keep doing stuff

Good luck.

In case you're interested

The author, is a retired Navy Navigating Officer serving for many years on tramp merchant ships plying trade all over the world. After the seafaring period of his life had come to an end he became actively involved in driving instructing, freelance selling numerous widely varied products and bookkeeping for other people,-all at the same time! While doing all that by day he took a job as a mobile security guard at night. His aim in life is to 'keep doing stuff'.

He loves all animals, especially his rescued Labrador and two adopted black cats.

His family is split between the USA and the UK and he enjoys travelling between the two countries whenever possible. He is actively engaged in charitable service, giving to and supporting the needy. He has been a member of three different Rotary International clubs (their motto being 'Service above Self'), and is currently a member of his local Lions International club. (their motto being 'We Serve'). He has previously been a Club President in both Rotary and Lions.

He started his writing some time ago when, in an unusual, moment of having nothing much to do, he thought writing a book or two might be a good way to fill in the gaps in a busy life. He had a few coloring books published before progressing into writing fiction and non-fiction books.

When not writing, he occupies himself in his favorite hobbies of computer building, model making and not very good photography, but above all, he diligently avoids procrastinating by keeping active and 'doing stuff'!

Now go and do
whatever it was
that you put off
or forgot.

Things that need doing	Done √

More things that need doing	Done √

Still more things that need doing	Done ✓

Notes for Action

More Notes for Action

DON'T think
about it anymore

just DO IT!

Dear reader.

Thank you so much for taking the time to read through this little book, and I hope that some if not all of the content has been helpful to you in your deliberations.

Stay happy, keep doing stuff and you will feel more and more satisfactorily accomplished.

Good luck.